The Dance of Differentiation

The Dance of Differentiation

Choreographing Inclusive Learning in Schools

DR TOM PORTA

amba
press

Published in 2024 by Amba Press, Melbourne, Australia
www.ambapress.com.au

Cover design: Tess McCabe
Internal design: Amba Press
Editor: Andrew Campbell

ISBN: 9781923116337 (pbk)
ISBN: 9781923116344 (ebk)

A catalogue record for this book is available from the National Library of Australia.

What your colleagues are saying

Regardless of where you are on your differentiation journey, this highly readable and richly informative book by Dr Tom Porta is a must-read. Quality insight from extensive research, unpacked in a digestible manner, challenges you to think about the *why* underpinning differentiation. Simultaneously, enriching information is shared on *how* to implement differentiation with liberal sprinklings of practical strategies frankly evaluated through a personal experience lens. The vast array of tools to gauge and respond to learner readiness elevates this book to handbook status for teachers keen to differentiate learning efficiently and effectively in their classrooms. The author passionately promotes the ideal of a whole-school approach where intentional differentiation is an integral piece of the school's pedagogical philosophy.

**Angeline Panayi-Motus, Business and Economics Teacher,
Seymour College**

Tom's expertise and knowledge of differentiation and the art of making it relevant to teachers is second to none. *The Dance of Differentiation* explains the steps and movements a skilled teacher will make in order to achieve inclusive education. Knowing that students will require different supports and instructions throughout a lesson is vital to the success of each and every student. This book is a must-read for every teacher, whether they have been in the classroom for many years or are just starting out.

Rebecca Mattinson, Teacher, Westminster School

This book is an invaluable resource for teachers at all stages of their career who have the desire to better their understanding and skills in differentiation and inclusive practices. Having had Tom as my teacher in high school, I can confidently say his passion and dedication to continually better the field of inclusive education extends well beyond the text in this book, reaching each and every student in his classroom. A highly recommended read that challenges the initial thinking around differentiation and provides readers with a guide to ensure a more inclusive education is delivered to our learners.

Elicia Baldwin, Teacher, Loreto College

In *The Dance of Differentiation*, Dr Tom Porta provides us with a nuanced and comprehensive approach to differentiation that offers practical guidance while also exploring the complex fields of learning and assessment. The central tenet of this book is that, by adopting a student-centred approach to teaching, teachers can use differentiation as a way to enhance the learning opportunities for all students, in all school settings. I commend this book for educators who seek to create inclusive and positive classroom cultures. Packed with research, tips, and strategies for support, it is a must-read for all educators – from beginner teachers right through to experienced school leaders.

Christopher Hudson, educational leader and author of
Leading Positive Classrooms

Dr Tom Porta's *The Dance of Differentiation* is a must-read for educators who want to take their differentiation skills to the next level. This book is packed with practical tips and examples on how to design and deliver lessons that meet the diverse needs of your students. You will learn how to use clear learning objectives, assessment strategies, and professional learning to enhance your differentiation practice. Tom also shows how school leaders can foster a culture of inclusion and excellence in their schools. This book is not just informative, but also inspiring and engaging. Don't miss this opportunity to learn from an expert and transform your teaching!

Angela Phillips, Director of Teaching, Westminster School

Contents

About the Author   ix

Acknowledgements   xi

A message to teachers: Stepping onto the stage   1

Introduction   5

Chapter 1   What is the dance of differentiation?   9

Chapter 2   The first steps of the dance   31

Chapter 3   Assessment as the opening move   57

Chapter 4   How *ready* are you to dance?   85

Chapter 5   Can I *interest* you in a *preferred* dance?   105

Chapter 6   Rhythmic innovations   125

Chapter 7   Stepping into confidence   145

Chapter 8   Dance partners   167

Conclusion   185

References   187

About the Author

Dr Tom Porta is a passionate educator, dedicating his professional career to promoting inclusion and inclusive education in school settings. Tom has been a teacher and school leader across state, Catholic and independent schools for the past decade, working to ensure inclusive practices, such as differentiation, are embedded in teachers' and school leaders' daily practices. In 2019, he was recognised as a certified Highly Accomplished Teacher by the Australian Institute of Teaching and School Leadership.

Tom studied for a Bachelor of Education, majoring in Biology and Psychology, and a Master of Special Education at Flinders University. In 2019, he embarked on a PhD through the University of Southern Queensland, focusing on senior-secondary teachers' attitudes towards, and self-efficacy in, differentiated instruction. Tom completed his PhD in 2023 and worked as a Lecturer in Initial and Continuing Education at Flinders University. As of 2024, Tom is a Lecturer in Education at the University of Adelaide.

Tom has published several academic papers in leading journals and is continuing research on inclusive classrooms.

Tom is currently on the board of the South Australian Chapter of the Australian Association of Special Education. He is an avid and lifelong learner, currently studying for a Diploma of Modern Languages in Italian at the University of New England.

Acknowledgements

First, I would like to acknowledge my publisher, Alicia Cohen, for recognising my vision in this book, enabling it to come to fruition. It has been an absolute delight to work with you and your team, and I am incredibly grateful for the opportunity. Thank you for seeing the importance of this book as an educational resource for teachers – we are only just starting to understand and work towards inclusive education, and this book contributes to that trajectory. I would also like to thank the wider team at Amba Press, for enabling my vision to come to fruition.

A continuing light that burns in me to be more inclusive and to promote inclusion comes from my cousin Kate. We lost you at the prime of your life – I often wonder how life might have been if you were here with us now. You have, however, a memory that lives on in my work on inclusion.

To my partner, Aaron (and fur baby, Flora), who likely knows by now that when I say I am going to slow down, it will not happen. Thank you for supporting me with every decision I make. You support my dreams in every way possible and it means the world to me.

To my family, thank you for your continued love, guidance and encouragement. I would not be where I am today without you.

To those who read my manuscript and provided me with feedback, thank you for ensuring that this book is practical and highly relevant to teachers across Australia, acting as a guide for effective differentiation. I appreciate the time and effort it took to review and I am deeply appreciative.

Finally, thanks go to you as the reader of this book. Whether you are a teacher, school leader or principal, or have some other vested interest in education, I know that you have picked up this book for the same reason I wrote it. I hope that you will be an advocate for differentiation and inclusive education in your school – that you will help colleagues to better their inclusive practices and skills in differentiation, leading to a more inclusive school system.

Stepping onto the stage

"If a man does not keep pace with his companions, perhaps it is
because he hears a different drummer. Let him step to the music
which he hears, however measured or far away."
– Henry David Thoreau

This is the book that I wish I had 10 years ago when I entered the world
of teaching as a scared pre-service teacher, hoping to make sure I could
bring out the best in all of my students – a book that would guide me to
better understand not only what differentiation is, but how to implement it
efficiently and effectively. Over the course of my career, I have seen teachers
differentiate really well, and I have seen teachers differentiate poorly or not
at all – propelling me to complete a PhD in this area, looking at the reasons
why teachers choose to differentiate or not. I found that teachers had varied
understandings of what differentiation was, but above all, many teachers
did not know how to implement it in ways that allowed them to utilise it
every day or with confidence.

I have been extremely lucky in that I have been inside many classrooms
throughout my career, observing and giving feedback to teachers to improve
their skills in differentiation and inclusive education practices. I first started
as a teacher aide during my university days, helping students and teachers
in differentiating curriculum, moving into various teaching and leadership
roles, and most recently, lecturing at Flinders University on inclusion and
diversity topics. I have also been lucky enough to work with some fantastic
colleagues who are highly skilled differentiators, crafting classrooms that
provide equitable learning experiences for all. I have learned a lot from
these teachers.

As I started to think about this book, I started wondering about all of the ways
teachers have been described in today's society. We hear these descriptions

while we are listening to a professional development session at the start of the school year. We are described as the facilitator, the collaborator, the planner, the juggler, the initiator... and so on. I don't believe, however, that these descriptions do our role justice. While we are many of these, we appear to dance between them at times, performing a sort of choreography of steps between each of them.

Aha... the dancer!

In the vibrant world of teaching, we as educators are choreographers, transforming our classrooms into dance floors of learning. In this journey, we do not just teach – we dance! We perform a symphony of strategies, moving in sync with the diverse rhythms of our students' minds.

Teaching, much like dance, is an art form, and in this book we delve into the intricate steps of a dance that educators know as differentiation. It is a dance where the melody of individuality resonates, where each step is tailored to honour the unique beats of every learner that steps into our classroom.

Just as the dancer adjusts their movements to match the music's tempo, teachers need to differentiate to suit each student's readiness, preferences, interests and strengths. This forward motion, the constant adjustment and alignment of dance, embodies the essence of differentiation.

Throughout these pages, you will discover the parallels between dance and differentiation. We set the stage, looking at how we can ensure our students all have access to high-quality curriculum and learning objectives. We explore how assessment becomes the initial sway, how planning acts as the choreographic masterpiece, and how instructional strategies mimic the fluidity of dance techniques. We will explore the role of technological advances in generative AI, which can be used to enhance our dancing, and deep-dive into professional learning methods to ensure all teachers make gains in differentiation. Lastly, we take the lens of school leaders as being crucial partners in the dance, in creating a culture of differentiation.

I invite you to immerse yourself in this metaphorical ballroom, to twirl with the ideas, and to find your rhythm in the dance of differentiation. Let's embark on this journey together, knowing that – just like in dance – the beauty lies not only in the final performance, but in the learning and refinement of every step along the way.

The fear of getting differentiation "wrong" was a driving force behind my PhD research. I wanted to better understand the challenges and enablers teachers were facing in implementing differentiation. After all, this is a framework that promotes inclusion, so why would you not utilise it for the betterment of your students? I have since learned that while differentiation is a skill, and there is certainly a right way to do it, you will only learn from making mistakes. You will find that many of the examples I highlight in this book are not of top-notch or high-quality differentiation. There are certainly some, but you will be exposed to my own personal challenges, mistakes and failures in differentiation. The professional dialogue I take you through will help you to become confident in this dance of differentiation.

So, as we take that first step onto the dance floor, let's embrace the music of diversity, celebrating the uniqueness of every learner and honing our craft as educators. Here's to the transformative power of this dance and to the magic it brings to our classrooms.

Let the dance begin!

Dr Tom Porta
www.drtomporta.com

Introduction

"To dance is to be out of yourself. Larger, more beautiful, more powerful." – Agnes de Mille

Differentiation is one of the most challenging, misunderstood and rewarding approaches to teaching I have taken throughout my whole career. I remember graduating from university having learned about differentiation, thinking, "How can I do this? How will I be able to do this in every lesson of every day to cater to the needs of my students?" I felt overwhelmed.

I can tell you here and now that the first few times I tried to implement differentiation, it did not go well. I felt that I was losing control of my classroom and that my role as the teacher was being diminished because students were moving all over the place, changing groups, having more independence in the classroom, which I felt I should not be giving. Perhaps this was because, as a student and as a pre-service teacher, I had observed many teachers teaching to the middle of the class, standing at the front and teaching in front of the whiteboard, while students sat in uniform rows and never moved from their spots. Interaction was minimal. This was not what I wanted from my classroom. It was not all doom and gloom, though, because I observed some outstanding teachers who differentiated incredibly well, and I could see the benefits this had on their students – this propelled me to want to be a better differentiator.

I realised that, to develop my skills in differentiation, I had to let go of some of the teaching practices that I had seen and were perhaps engrained into me. In particular, I had to let go of teaching at the front of the classroom, lecturing to students from the whiteboard, hoping all my students understood my instruction. This was what I had observed too much during my university practicums. I had to let myself make mistakes but really be willing to give different differentiation practices a go. I recognised, along the way, that differentiation was more than just a set of strategies – that I needed to change my whole philosophy of teaching, recognising that I wanted all my students, no matter their knowledge and skills, to be included in my classroom and to be challenged. This is where I realised that differentiation is really a way of life in teaching. Differentiation is a philosophy linked to inclusive education, and the two work in partnership with one another, ensuring all students, no matter the diversity they bring to the classroom, have their needs met.

One of the most important things I want to say about differentiation, and I reiterate this many times throughout the book, is that differentiation is one way of achieving inclusive education. Differentiation should not be utilised alone – in fact, differentiation really needs to be utilised alongside Universal Design for Learning and other teaching pedagogies. Graham (2023), in her second edition of *Inclusive Education for the 21st Century*, outlined that providing adjustments to student learning should not be as an add-on and that teachers should not plan to the middle of the class, adding on adjustments for students, so they can access what the rest of the class is doing. Instead, accessibility needs to be considered at the very beginning, as all students have the right to access their age-equivalent and grade level curriculum. Therefore, as you begin to take this journey for differentiation, be sure it does not take away from providing universally designed and accessible classrooms.

This book serves as a handbook, guide, reflective journal, challenger of thinking, and collection of personal stories to assist both the novice and the adept in implementing differentiation into their classroom. This book is designed not just for the classroom teacher, but for the school leader who is looking for ways to enable differentiation to gain traction in their site. I highlight examples of differentiation in practice, which was something I so desperately wanted when I started my differentiation journey. This book, however, is by no means exhaustive. By that, I mean that I highlight a selection of ways you can differentiate to help you build confidence. Start small. It takes time. Be ready to feel uncomfortable and be taken out of your comfort zone as you begin this journey. You may not agree with everything I say in this book, and it is designed to challenge your thinking and ways of teaching. After all, if I did not challenge you, then you may not see a reason to change or adapt your teaching methodology and practices.

I want you to make a promise to yourself as you read this book – that this book is not going to become one of those books that you read a few chapters of and put on your shelf for the next 15 years; that instead, you will actively trial or adapt some of the aspects in your classroom. Set yourself a goal of reading a chapter in the space of a few weeks, perhaps individually or with colleagues. Working with colleagues to achieve differentiation is discussed extensively in this book, because they keep you accountable, so reach out to someone and have them come on this dancing journey with you. I know it is scary, but I have faith in you. You picked this book up for a reason! So take it with you and don't let it sit in the bookshelf collecting dust.

This book starts by outlining what differentiation is, and how differentiation fits into the bigger picture of inclusion and student diversity. This is crucial and will help you to understand the philosophy and principles behind differentiation, rather than seeing it as a series of strategies for implementation. I take you through how you can draw upon the Version 9 Australian Curriculum as a starting point for your differentiation decisions, further looking at ways you can determine what students know, understand and can do, as well as their interests and preferences in learning. You will explore ways of differentiating based on student data collected.

Furthermore, I am a firm believer in differentiating efficiently and effectively – utilising technology and resources that allow you to achieve this; therefore, you will explore the use of artificial intelligence in helping you to differentiate. Similarly, a key component of getting differentiation right is ensuring that you are not doing it alone; hence, you will explore ways that schools and school leaders can enable you to become better differentiators through the way they approach professional development and school policies.

As I write this book, Australia is in the midst of a teacher crisis (Cawte, 2020; Waley, 2022), and teachers are leaving the profession in droves – with an estimated 30 to 50 percent of teachers leaving within the first five years of teaching (Weldon, 2018). Furthermore, fewer people are entering the teacher workforce (Arnup & Bowles, 2016; Heffernan et al., 2019). Knowing that teachers are feeling the pressure, experiencing exhaustion, stress, burnout and heavy workloads (Heffernan et al., 2022), I wanted to write a practical handbook that steps out some of the elements of differentiation in a bite-sized way – a book that should not be seen as an *add-on* or another thing to do, but as something that can help you to become more efficient and effective in your teaching practices. I believe that all teachers want the best for their students, and that teachers try their best to achieve this, often leaving them feeling burnt out. Use this book to assist you to achieve this more effectively.

This book offers you a chance to reflect after each chapter, as well as a series of supporting activities. As I introduce you to key concepts and aspects of differentiation, I provide you with the opportunity to apply these and link them back to your own classrooms. Hence, as you make your way through this book, you should, in fact, have created a range of differentiated lessons you can apply in your teaching. Start a book club or professional learning community with some colleagues – work away a chapter at a time and apply what you have learned and come back and share with one another. Sharing successes and failures is all part of the process of developing confidence in differentiation. I know you will be bold in this way.

As you engage in this book, you will develop a deeper understanding of the following AITSL standards:

1.2 Understand how students learn
1.3 Students with diverse linguistic, cultural, religious and socioeconomic backgrounds
1.5 Differentiate teaching to meet the specific learning needs of students across the full range of abilities
1.6 Strategies to support full participation of students with disability
2.1 Content and teaching strategies of the teaching area
3.2 Plan, structure and sequence learning programs
3.3 Use teaching strategies
6.2 Engage in professional learning and improve practice.

Last, while this book focuses on differentiation, I take you through a journey in Chapter 1 on how differentiation fits into the bigger picture of inclusive education. Therefore, some key documents that you may find useful as you extend your knowledge in inclusive education are outlined below. I encourage you to familiarise yourself with these, as they will only enhance your understanding of differentiation. These documents further highlight the commitment we have, and the rights of our students, in meeting their diverse learning needs.

- Disability Discrimination Act 1992
- Disability Standards for Education 2005
- General Comment No. 4 on Article 24: Right to Inclusive Education by the United Nations 2016
- Queensland Department of Education Inclusive Education Policy Statement 2018
- The Alice Springs (Mparntwe) Education Declaration 2019.

CHAPTER 1

What is the dance of differentiation?

"There are three steps you have to complete to become a professional dancer: learn to dance, learn to perform, and learn how to cope with injuries."

- DAVID GERE

Learning objectives

By the end of this chapter:

- Teachers will understand that differentiation is one philosophical approach to teaching that contributes to inclusive education.
- Teachers will know the elements of the differentiated instruction framework that can be applied at various times through classroom teaching.
- Teachers will be able to select elements of the differentiated instruction framework to cater to student diversity in their classroom.

Never in the history of education has there been a greater need to be educated in ways to be more inclusive, and to cater for the diversity that exists in the grand ballroom that is our classrooms. Student diversity has become ever so prevalent, taking centre stage in the last decade (Sun & Xiao, 2021). The importance of inclusion and inclusive education has heightened too, with the most recent Australian report from the Teacher Education Expert Panel (Australian Government, 2023b) finding that many teachers do not know what to do to be more inclusive in their classrooms. I consider this finding scary and I wonder what this means for the students in our classrooms who think differently, have different needs to one another, perhaps struggle in their learning, or require more support. Hence, there are two current and significant challenges facing you as a teacher:

1. How do you respond to student diversity in the classroom?
2. How can you create successful and inclusive learning environments to promote achievement of all students (Gheyssens et al., 2020).

In this chapter you will explore what diversity is and how it exists in all classrooms, regardless of whether students have a specific label, diagnosis or identified learning need or not. Your classroom is likely very diverse already, and may include students with learning difficulties or learning disabilities (such as dyslexia), students on the autism spectrum, students with physical disabilities, gifted students, and students with mental health concerns. These labels, while important, are something you should move away from as you begin to differentiate (Porta & Todd, 2023). This is because you do not want them clouding the way you differentiate – for example, always assuming that the students with disabilities will have lower readiness in knowledge, understanding or skills and therefore only providing these students with lower challenge.

I preface this chapter too by saying that while you explore inclusion and what inclusive education means, you are merely skimming the surface here. There is much research and debate about inclusive education and what this means in schools. I encourage you to look at works by Professor Linda Graham if you are interested in looking more deeply at what true inclusive education looks like. Gone are the days of *teaching to the middle* – providing one method of teaching instruction and hoping that all students in the class will be engaged, challenged and grow academically. This practice does not allow for equity of inclusion in education, and planning for diversity through universally designed classrooms is needed and required in your classrooms. Over the years, teachers have taught students with diverse learning needs in many ways, and some of these practices still exist in today's classrooms. Students with diverse learning needs are often removed from the mainstream classroom, or are present but working with teachers' aides, or working on content that is not challenging (Graham, 2019) – *busy work*, as I like to term it. The sad truth is that I still see many instances of teachers teaching to the middle (in my professional opinion), often leaving students with diverse needs behind. This was what I was exposed to during my observations as a pre-service teacher, and I honestly believed that this was what teaching was, with the occasional differentiated lesson. Hence, I can understand why many teachers do teach to the middle, because they have been exposed to such practices and do not know how to confidently implement strategies that move away from this.

As this practice continues, and the years go on, the gap only gets wider for these students, and teachers are left more confused about how to bridge that gap (Harlin et al., 2009). I do not believe that teachers teach to the middle out of choice, but rather because they may be scared or unsure of what to do and how to do it! There is also a perception among many teachers that they must provide students with the same instruction, learning materials, conditions etc. for their education to be considered fair (Porta & Todd, 2022). I take you through fairness and equity throughout this book.

Take a student who perhaps has some difficulties with working memory and retaining necessary information, taking longer to retrieve the information. Put them in a test condition and give them the same time and conditions as everyone else. Will they be successful? Likely not. Many of you will be familiar with what fairness looks like in education, but Figure 1 describes it perfectly. Ultimately teachers need to be striving for equity in their classrooms over fairness. Think of a student who wears glasses. Do you ask them to take off their glasses because other students do not have them and it could be seen as an advantage? Of course not! That student needs those glasses to see – it allows them to be successful based on the diverse needs that they have. Differentiation is just one philosophical approach and practice that recognises and embraces equity in education. You may be used to providing a classroom that is fair, and this is where you may need to be open to shifting your thinking.

Figure 1: Fairness in education

Our Education System

For education to be equitable, you need to create inclusion and inclusive classrooms and schools. Inclusive education is not the same as special education, which traditionally relies upon models of segregation or integration, rather than an inclusive approach. In my opinion, special education is a very outdated term and should be avoided as you move towards more inclusive means of education. I do use this term in the book a few times, but it is a term that I don't agree with. Put quite simply, inclusive education is good education (Richler, 2012) and is the process of increasing participation in, and decreasing exclusion from, the curriculum, culture and community of mainstream schools (Booth & Ainscow, 2002). The United Nations (2016, p. 4) outlined inclusion incredibly well by saying that:

Inclusion involves a process of systemic reform embodying changes and modification in content, teaching methods, approaches, structures, and strategies in education to overcome barriers with a vision serving to provide all students of the relevant age range with an equitable and participatory learning experience and environment that best corresponds to their requirements and preferences.

Every student, no matter their learning needs, is entitled to an inclusive classroom environment. Figure 2 highlights the key differences between inclusion, exclusion, segregation and integration. You typically see segregation in models such as special schools – where students with complex needs are taught in completely different settings that are not considered mainstream (Graham, 2019) – and there is much research showing that segregation is harmful (Oh-Young & Filler, 2015). Similarly, many schools still practise integration practices (Graham, 2019). In my experience, nearly all the schools I have worked with and for follow an integration approach, believing they are being inclusive.

Some of you reading this book will have a very clear understanding of what inclusion is and what it looks like, and some of you may not. In my first year of teaching, I became the inclusive education coordinator for a small school – a role that was designed to help teachers be more inclusive in their classrooms. I interviewed all the staff and asked them to tell me whether or not they felt they were inclusive in their classrooms. The majority of them said they were. I was really excited about this – I thought "Great, we can harness this to influence others to do the same". I was, however, shocked to find that inclusion was not what was actually happening. Teachers thought they were being inclusive, when in fact, they were taking an integrative and segregative approach in their classrooms. Students with diverse needs were certainly in the mainstream classroom, but were often given a series of booklets or worksheets to complete in the back corner, while the teacher taught to the rest of their students. They were given *busy work*.

These students were often encouraged to leave the classroom and go to the learning centre, a room dedicated for students with learning difficulties and disabilities to do their work, either individually or with a teacher aide. I watched those students lose motivation, not be challenged academically, and I could see the academic gap widen. The expectations of these students were constantly being lowered, to the point where the students themselves felt they could not finish school or work in meaningful employment. This led to a cycle where teachers became frustrated because they felt the student could not achieve the year level equivalent, thus widening the gap for the student and making the teacher more frustrated about how to lessen the gap.

Over the course of my teaching career, I have seen this integration model in most schools – to which many will argue that the mainstream classroom is too challenging for students with learning difficulties, disabilities and other diverse learning needs, and not suitable for them. Even as I started to undertake my PhD research, I was shocked to find that, as students were moving into senior-secondary years, their pathways and subject selections were being limited because many teachers felt these students could not achieve in classes such as higher-level mathematics or higher-level English subjects (Porta, 2023). We know, though, from decades and decades of research, that including all students, no matter their learning needs, in the mainstream classroom has significant short- and long-term benefits for *all* students, not just those with diverse learning needs (Graham, 2019; Hehir et al., 2016). Some of these benefits include: greater positive behaviour, academic development, increased independence, patience, trust and acceptance of diversity, better communication and language development (Cologon, 2022). Differentiation is one way that you can achieve inclusive education (Jarvis, 2015).

Figure 2: Inclusive education compared to exclusion, segregation and integration

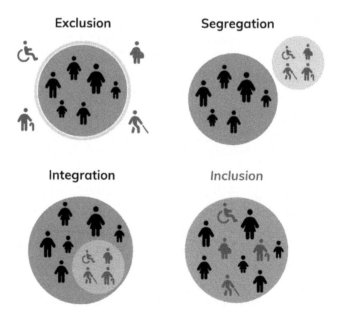

As teachers in Australia, you have a responsibility to differentiate the curriculum and instruction for students. The Australian Professional Standards for Teaching (APST) created by the Australian Institute for Teaching and School Leadership, state that teachers need to "know their students and how they learn" and that (at a graduate level), teachers need to "demonstrate knowledge and understanding of strategies for differentiating teaching to meet the specific needs of students across the full range of abilities" (Australian Institute for Teaching and School Leadership, 2017). It is part of the job of teachers to differentiate; however, this responsibility does not make it easier to differentiate. In fact, I felt a tension many times myself where I knew I should have been differentiating, but could not, because of fear of the unknown, fear of getting it wrong, or simply not knowing where to start. I would often wonder, "Who am I supposed to be differentiating for? Is differentiation just providing a few students in the class with some further resources? Should it be just for my special education students?" (This is a view held by many teachers (Porta & Todd, 2023)). However, as the APST say, differentiation is to meet the needs of students across a full range of abilities – and this is where student diversity comes in.

What is student diversity?

Terminology in Australian education systems is rife – by that, I mean that different states and territories use different terms to describe diversity. We see students termed as having special needs (terminology I do not like!), additional needs, learning difficulties and learning disabilities, and this terminology is often used interchangeably in different areas across Australia (Todd et al., 2022). Even now, 10 years into teaching and a PhD later, I still find myself confused by terminology as to what constitutes student diversity, learning difficulties, etc. So, I sympathise with those of you who struggle to distinguish between these terms, because I was once just as confused.

However, think of student diversity as an umbrella term, something that encompasses many different aspects – I will unpack this further. The Australian Curriculum takes a narrow lens when looking at what diversity exists in our classrooms (Australian Curriculum, Assessment and Reporting Authority, 2023d). It states that students with disability, those who are gifted and talented, and those who have English as an additional language or dialect are considered diverse students. Diversity is, however, much more than this, and you need to look beyond the students who perhaps have a label, diagnosis or identified learning need, or are a part of a group, such as students with disabilities, to understand diversity. We are all different and unique, and students bring with them different skills and capacities to the classroom (Sands et al., 2000). You need to move away from defining students are being part of a certain group, as you run the risk of providing students with a *one-size-fits-all* mentality (Abawi et al., 2019), providing blanket strategies based on preconceived notions (Porta & Todd, 2023) – for example, providing scaffolding for all students who are on the autism spectrum, even though they may not all need scaffolding. Abawi et al. (2019) outline five factors that contribute to diversity, shown in Figure 3. So, while we can understand student diversity as referring to students who perhaps have a label attached to them, you need to look beyond the label. As you explore differentiation throughout this book, you will see that, while labels and identified learning needs can guide you in how to differentiate (Porta & Todd, 2023), differentiation strategies can allow you to look past the label, focusing on the students themselves in a more holistic manner and on where they are at academically at that point in time.

Figure 3: Factors contributing to diversity

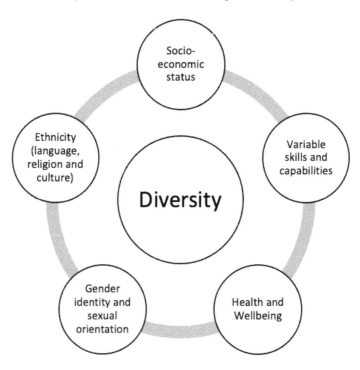

SOURCE: ABAWI ET AL. (2019).

Defining differentiation

If you have ever wondered what differentiation *actually* is, you would not be alone. In fact, there are numerous studies that highlight teacher confusion about what differentiation is, how it is implemented, and how it has become quite misused in teaching with many misconceptions (Dack, 2019; Tomlinson, 2014) – often termed as adjustments, modifications, individualised or personalised learning, etc. You may have heard differentiation termed as differentiated instruction, given that, over the years, these two terms have been used interchangeably (Scarparolo & Subban, 2023). I will be using the term differentiation throughout most of this book, as the term differentiation is best described as a philosophical and pedagogical approach to creating inclusive classrooms and responding to student diversity (Scarparolo & Subban, 2023), rather than differentiated instruction. Differentiation allows you, as the teacher, to move away from a one-size-fits-all approach to teaching and learning, recognising that your students are all different in many ways and that you can engage them by understanding their readiness, utilising their interests, and allowing students to learn in ways they prefer, to increase their motivation (Tomlinson, 2014). Differentiation is about being *proactive* and *responsive* to students' needs (Berman et al., 2023). That is to say, differentiation requires some active planning on your part in its initial setup, and you need to make changes to your teaching program, depending on where your students are at and how they are progressing.

Think of a dancer, someone who has perhaps been dancing the tango for a very long time, who not only choreographs each move in advance but also remains exquisitely responsive to the music's nuances. Similarly, effective teaching through differentiation involves a seamless blend of preparation and responsiveness. Teachers, much like dancers, need to plan their lessons to ensure they have a set of steps tailored to meet the diverse rhythms of their students' needs. Just as a dance improvises, however, a teacher observes and adapts in real time, changing their strategies to match a variety of diverse needs. This proactive and responsive interplay in differentiation ensures a harmonious educational performance.

Often, when I work with schools and we try to define what differentiation is, it can be easier to do so when we look at what differentiation *is not*. The list below includes some of the common misconceptions. As you read these, take note of whether you hold, or once held, some of these misconceptions. I, for one, used to think differentiation was just a series of strategies, not realising it is a philosophy of teaching.

Common misconceptions of differentiation

- Differentiation means I need to prepare 25 different lessons for 25 different students.
- Differentiation addresses learning styles.
- Differentiation does not align with standardised assessments.
- Differentiation means always grouping students.
- Differentiation is based on ability.
- Differentiation is only for students with special needs or gifted students.
- Differentiation is just a set of strategies.
- Differentiation is teaching down to some students and teaching up to others.
- Differentiation is individualised learning.

ADAPTED FROM DACK (2019) AND TOMLINSON (2022).

Many will argue that "Differentiation takes time to implement" is a misconception. However, I disagree with this… to an extent. Just as dancing takes time to master – you put in the practice and the hours to perfect the dance, and the dance soon becomes second nature to you. This is how I feel about differentiation. It takes time to initially become skilled in and confident in, but the more you practise it and live by its philosophy, the easier it becomes. I think it is unrealistic to believe that differentiation does not take time, because it does. That being said, there is often a payoff in this time investment. Later in the book I talk about learning menus for student interests and learning preferences and my use of them. They took significant time in planning, but allowed me more time to work and support individual students as students were working on the learning menus.

Many of the misconceptions above have likely arisen from earlier definitions of differentiation. In fact, differentiation has been around since as early as the 1960s, and was known as *differential learning* (Ward, 1961), used for students identified as gifted and in need of extra challenge in their learning. The theme of differentiation being for gifted students continued into the 1990s, when it was determined that, for teachers, it is not acceptable to treat everyone the same (Tomlinson et al., 1996). After all, we are not all the same, so why should we be treated as such?

Definitions of differentiation have evolved since the 1990s, and while there are many frameworks and definitions for differentiation, such as Westwood's five ways of differentiation (Westwood, 2016), the most well-known framework for differentiation is by Carol Tomlinson (2014). Her full framework can be seen below (Figure 4), and I will unpack the core principles and key elements of this framework as they will be referred to as you start to step out how to implement differentiation. Do not let this framework overwhelm you at this early stage in your differentiation journey. I will show you how you can utilise some of these elements in your classroom; however, it is important to understand the philosophy of differentiation in the first instance, as it is much more than just a set of strategies to be implemented.

Figure 4: Differentiated instruction framework by Tomlinson

Differentiation

is a teacher's **proactive** response to learner needs

shaped by **mindset**

and guided by general principles of differentiation

An environment that encourages and supports learning	Quality curriculum	Assessment that informs teaching and learning	Instruction that responds to student variance	Leading students and managing routines

Teachers can differentiate through

Content The information and ideas students grapple with to reach the learning goals	**Process** How students take in and make sense of the content	**Product** How students show what they know, understand, and can do	**Affect/ Environment** The climate or tone of the classroom

according to the student's

Readiness A student's proximity to specified learning goals	**Interests** Passions, affinities, kinships that motivate learning	**Learning Profile** Preferred approaches to learning

through a variety of instructional strategies, such as

Learning/Interest Centers • RAFTs • Graphic Organizers • Scaffolded Reading/Writing
Intelligence Preferences • Tiered Assignments • Learning Contracts • Menus • Tic-Tac-Toe
Complex Instruction • Independent Projects • Expression Options • Small-Group Instruction

SOURCE: TOMLINSON (2014).

Core principles of differentiation

As I have already established, differentiation takes a proactive and responsive approach to addressing students' diverse needs. Differentiation is about recognising that each student brings with them a different set of learning needs and that you as teachers can meet these needs in a variety of ways (Tomlinson, 2014). These needs change all the time, and you need to keep track of what they are, so you can address them accordingly. Similarly, differentiation is built on the premise that teachers can differentiate quality curriculum (Tomlinson, 2014; Tomlinson & Borland, 2022). Using the appropriate space in Supporting Activity 1 (page 29), outline what you think is meant by the term *high-quality curriculum*. What do you think a high-quality curriculum consists of?

As you progress through this book, you will see that I am utilising Version 9 of the Australian Curriculum (Australian Curriculum, Assessment and Reporting Authority, 2023a) as the basis for differentiation. This is because the Version 9 Australian Curriculum is the mandated curriculum in most states and territories across Australia, and has the characteristics of a high-quality curriculum. Tomlinson and Moon (2013) argued that a quality curriculum should have three things:

1. It should have clear goals for what students should know, understand and be able to do.
2. It should allow for deep understanding of the content, not just memorisation of content.
3. It should engage students in the process of learning.

As you delve into Chapter 2, I will step you through how you can take the Version 9 Australian Curriculum and create meaningful learning objectives that engage students, allowing them to think more deeply on a conceptual level, and determine students' readiness in relation to these learning objectives.

Understanding content, process, product and environment

One of the features of differentiation is content differentiation, which consists of the essential knowledge, understanding and skills that are being taught (Tomlinson, 1997). Teachers differentiate content based on how ready students are to learn, their specific interests, or information supplied by learning preferences. Content is what you ask students to learn, and it is more common to differentiate how students access the content, rather than the content itself. Many teachers, particularly those who teach in senior-secondary schooling, feel pressure in having to *get through the content* (Porta, 2023), leading them to express difficulties in what content to cover at certain points during the teaching semester or year. The aim here is not to remove content – remember you want to uphold a quality curriculum, but you may change how students access the content. Tomlinson (2022) outlined that teachers can differentiate content by providing such content through readings, diagrams, field trips, videos, news sources and first-hand experiences.

In contrast, differentiation by process is the way that students make sense of content, with the differentiation of that process involving activities – for example, small group discussions or activities, in-class practice, or use of graphic organisers. Differentiation by process often takes the form of flexible grouping strategies (Tomlinson, 2014) such as mixed readiness, similar readiness, or interest and learner preference groupings. In my work, I have differentiated process more than I have differentiated content or product.

Similarly, differentiation by product refers to how students demonstrate their understanding and is often realised through teachers setting tasks where students can show their learning in a variety of ways. Teachers will often adapt pace, terminology and type of assessment as a means of differentiating product. Products are usually summative assessments (Tomlinson, 2022) – those that are assessed on criteria with grades applied. For the Version 9 Australian Curriculum, summative assessments usually determine where students are in relation to the achievement standards.

In essence, the factors of content, process and product are similarly treated in differentiation, providing a variety of ways that students can acquire content and make sense of the ideas explored, so that each student can learn effectively (Tomlinson, 2001) and meet the same learning objectives. The image in Figure 5 highlights, in a very simplistic manner, how teachers can apply differentiation in their classrooms. You may take your students in different directions over the course of the lesson, but ultimately, they all reach the same end point. This is true for dancing – in many dance styles, there is no right way to dance, and people can take many different steps and dance to different rhythms. Ultimately, though, it does not matter how the dance was stepped, because each performance is unique. You will explore content, process and product in more detail as you progress through the steps of differentiation and learn to practically apply these in a variety of ways. There is, however, another way you can differentiate the classroom, and this is through the environment. Teachers can set the tone of the classroom in a variety of ways, such as by ensuring that students feel welcomed and valued, and helping students recognise that the classroom is a safe space to learn in – with both successes and failures.

Figure 5: Dancing to the tune of differentiation

Understanding readiness, interests and learner preferences

Firstly, no, I have not made a spelling error in this heading – you may have noticed a difference between Figure 4, which references learner profile, and my heading, which indicates learner preferences. In 2014, Tomlinson's framework for differentiation indicated that teachers could differentiate according to a student's learner profile – a more fixed way of thinking about students. More recently, she adapted her framework to change learner profile to learner preferences (Tomlinson, 2022), which we will explore later on. The term learner profile suggested that students' learn in a certain way without this changing, while learner preferences recognises that students may demonstrate their learning in preferred ways, and that these preferences can change over time.

In my opinion, the most important way you can differentiate is by differentiating content, process or product, according to a student's readiness levels. Readiness refers to how ready a student is to learn a particular concept, skill or content in the lesson or unit, sometimes known as their entry point (Tomlinson, 2014). For example, when I taught Year 11 nutrition in 2023, I knew that my students had different readiness levels when I was teaching them about carbohydrates. Some students were completing vocational courses in sport and nutrition, so they already knew what carbohydrates were; however, some students only knew carbohydrates as something that "made you fat" – a superficial understanding of this content. Therefore, they had varying readiness levels in relation to what they knew and understood about carbohydrates.

When I run professional development with schools, a question that gets raised by a lot of teachers is "What is the difference between readiness and ability?" In differentiation, we try to avoid the term ability, as ability suggests that a student's capacity to learn is somehow fixed – that it can never really change. Take my earlier example of my nutrition class and learning about carbohydrates: those students who had high readiness in relation to carbohydrates demonstrated quite a bit of knowledge. If I had assumed that they had high readiness for all concepts and content covered throughout the year, such as with fats or protein, then I would have been taking an approach that was more fixed, and therefore based on ability. This would be the same if I were to always assume that my students who had low readiness in one area had low readiness in all other areas too. I see this a lot in schools. Many teachers will assume that their "A" grade students have high readiness, and their "C" or "D" grade students have low readiness, always providing the low-readiness group with less challenge compared to the high-readiness group. Even when I conducted my research for my PhD, teachers often referred to their students by the grade level they achieved, talking about their A, B, C and D grade students. I want to encourage you to move away from this fixed type of practice, to not *box in* your students. The challenge here lies in determining student readiness in an ongoing manner – which we will explore more in later chapters when we discuss assessment.

Why readiness matters is crucial. There is much research in the field of educational psychology that shows that if tasks are too demanding for students, or provide little to no challenge, their academic achievement will be hindered (Vygotsky, 1978, 1987). This theory is very much based on Vygotsky's "zone of proximal development" (Vygotsky, 1978), as depicted in Figure 6. Vygotsky described the zone of proximal development as the level of potential development a learner can have when guided correctly by a peer or adult, which sits between what a student can do comfortably and what a student cannot do unaided. Differentiation allows teachers to assist learners who have difficulty grasping a concept, by implementing curriculum and instructional strategies to help them to understand and proceed at their own pace, moving them into the zone where they are able to accomplish what is asked of them, while providing them with some challenge. You might think of this like Goldilocks and the three bears – the zone of proximal development is the porridge that is *just right*.

Figure 6: Zone of proximal development

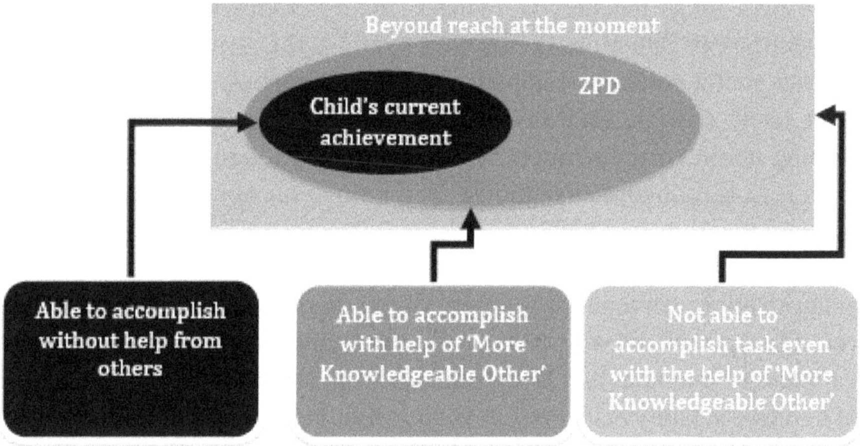

While teachers can differentiate by readiness, teachers can also differentiate content, process and/or product through students' interests. In doing so, students become more motivated to learn and often are more creative (Tomlinson, 2022). Similarly, they can share their interests with others, further connecting their interests to the classroom. Our ultimate goal is to get students engaged in the classroom, so why not connect the things they like into the tasks and instruction you provide?

Lastly, you can differentiate content, process and/or product by learner preferences (Tomlinson, 2022). It is more common to differentiate product by learner preferences, allowing students to demonstrate what they know in a way that they prefer (Dulfer, 2019). For example, some students prefer to demonstrate what they know through oral means, or by utilising technological applications like Canva or OneNote. You will explore both interests and learner preferences in more detail as you start to dance with differentiation.

What I have provided so far is a brief introduction to the elements of differentiation and where this fits within the greater scheme of inclusion and diversity. While I have outlined the principles and key areas of the differentiation framework developed by Tomlinson (2014), you have hopefully come to understand that differentiation is complex and multifaceted. Differentiation is not just a set of strategies, it is a philosophical approach that is underpinned by many principles that *inform* the differentiation practices you use. Tomlinson (2014, p. 25) called these "the three pillars of effective differentiation", and they can be seen in Figure 7. Differentiation is not something that you choose to use selectively or for individual students. Throughout my professional career, I have often heard teachers say, "I differentiated for that student last week" or "I differentiated for that student a few times". My response is to question this and say that this is not actually differentiation. To differentiate effectively, you have to adopt the mindset of trying to achieve inclusive education (Jarvis, 2015), knowing that students will require different supports and instruction at varying times in your classroom – meaning that you cannot just teach to the middle. Another key principle, which you will see in Chapter 3, is the use of ongoing assessment to inform your differentiation decisions. As you progress through the book, keep in mind the following:

1. You can differentiate by content, process and/or product, according to
2. students' current level of readiness, current interests and current learner preferences.

I use the word "current" because it is your job to keep up with your students' current readiness, interests and learner preferences, to create an effectively differentiated classroom.

Figure 7: Three pillars to effective differentiation

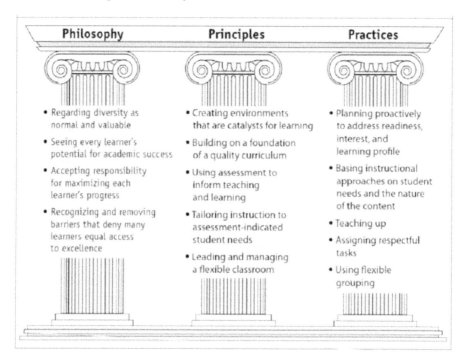

SOURCE: TOMLINSON (2014).

Multitiered systems of support

Before you start to look at actually implementing differentiation, it is important to understand where differentiation fits within the multitiered systems of support framework (MTSS), which is becoming increasingly common in schools as a means to guide how they approach academic and behavioural interventions (Barker et al., 2022). MTSS is made up of three key areas, known as tiers (Banks, 2022). These are outlined in Figure 8. Tier 1 refers to the universal supports you provide to *all* students in the classroom. All students are entitled to the universal supports and instruction in tier 1, and this is where differentiation falls. Teachers provide a differentiated learning environment to all students in their classrooms. There is much research that shows that when universal supports are put in place, like differentiation, then you see a reduction in the number of students moving into tiers 2 and 3 (Bambara et al., 2015), where they require more targeted approaches or intervention. It is crucial to note that differentiation is not intervention, as I established earlier in this chapter; differentiation is for all students.

Tier 2 involves teaching practices and interventions that are for select groups of students, who require more support. Traditionally, we have seen students in this tier who perhaps have disabilities or struggles in literacy and numeracy removed from the mainstream classroom for remediation or other intervention, such as formal intervention programs. The aim here, however, in striving to achieve inclusive education, is to address tier 2 concerns within the mainstream classroom. Tier 2 is typically for a small number of students in a classroom, between 5 and 15 percent (Banks, 2022). While differentiation is a tier 1 practice, I would argue that differentiation can assist you in your approach to tier 2. I will discuss this later when we look at flexible grouping and co-teaching strategies. Lastly, tier 3, which consists of approximately 2–5 percent of students (Banks, 2022), involves very individualised and intensive support for students who may be of serious concern both academically and behaviourally.

Figure 8: Multitiered systems of support

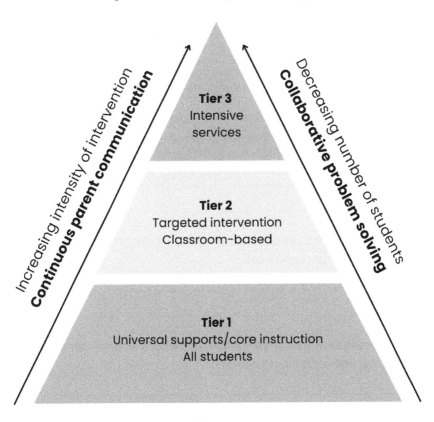

SOURCE: AMERICAN ACADEMY (N.D.).

Chapter summary and reflection

This chapter has established the link between differentiation, inclusive education, and addressing student diversity. I have outlined the framework of differentiation, as outlined by Carol Tominson in 2014, as a way of understanding that differentiation is more than just a set of strategies and practices – it is a philosophical approach to teaching that is guided by many principles. We have seen that differentiation is *one* way to achieve inclusive education and classrooms. Furthermore, we have explored the types of differentiation that you can select from, looking at how differentiation fits within the multitiered systems of support framework.

Take a moment now to reflect on your learning from this chapter, through the four steps outlined below. The purpose of this reflection tool is to get you thinking about your own teaching philosophy and how you may need to adapt your thinking to allow yourself to engage in differentiation.

1. **Do.** Describe your experiences with differentiation thus far. How have you differentiated in the past?

    _____

    _____

2. **Reflect.** How did you feel about your experiences in differentiation? What worked and what areas would you like to improve in? What were some of the misconceptions you held that have now been dispelled?

    _____

    _____

3. **Plan.** What will you do differently when adopting a differentiated approach to your classroom?

    _____

    _____

4. **Implement.** Outline one goal you would like to achieve when adopting a differentiated approach.

    _____

    _____

Supporting Activity 1

What is meant by the term "high-quality curriculum"? What do you think a high-quality curriculum consists of?

CHAPTER 2

The first steps of the dance

"When you dance, your purpose is not to get to a certain place on the floor. It's to enjoy each step along the way."

– WAYNE DYER

Figure 9: Backwards by design

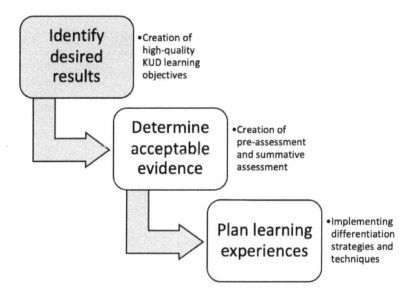

The importance of "backwards by design"

Over the course of this chapter, and the next, we will be outlining an "understanding by design" approach to differentiation by Wiggins and McTighe (2011) and Tomlinson and McTighe (2006), as depicted above. Understanding by design is also known as "backwards by design". This chapter will focus on identifying desired results. Essentially, you will be working backwards, starting with the curriculum, to design your differentiated lessons and unit plans. You may even be taking this approach in your planning of lessons and units already without even knowing it.

Taking an understanding by design or backwards by design approach allows you to make student learning more purposeful and to see the bigger picture of where each of your lessons fits within the overarching goals of your unit planning (Tomlinson & McTighe, 2006; Wiggins & McTighe, 2005, 2011). It forces you to see the bigger picture of where your lessons fit within the mandated curriculum and in your unit plans. Furthermore, the understanding by design approach allows you to focus on teaching and assessing for understanding and on how that understanding can transfer across multiple learning areas, rather than focusing directly on content.

As you go through the steps of differentiation, utilising an understanding by design approach, you may feel that this is quite rigid, given that there are a number of steps to be taken. Lean into this in the initial stages and for the first few times you begin to implement differentiation. I promise you that, as you develop confidence in these steps, they will become second nature to you, becoming more natural and less rigid. This approach to planning and teaching will give you a more accurate understanding of what your students know, understand and can do, as well as what *you* as the teacher want your students to know, understand and be able to do. You can also be confident that you are covering the mandated curriculum, ensuring students are exposed to their relevant year level content.

Now, I know the realistic nature of teaching. Was every one of my lessons planned out using the understanding by design approach? Did I have neatly crafted learning objectives for every one of my lessons? Of course not, particularly at the beginning of my teaching career! However, I wish I had! There were times, especially during a seven-lesson day, when I was writing my lesson plan on a sticky note, or even walking in blindly to the lesson, creating my learning objectives on the spot. You do what you can with the time you have. When I started taking an understanding by design approach in my unit planning, however, the benefit was that even if I was in a rush to a lesson, or I needed to be adaptive and change the focus of the lesson, I had a clear understanding of what I wanted my students to develop and the knowledge I wanted to deepen. In other words, I knew I had a good grasp on what I wanted my students to know, understand and be able to do. Understanding by design also meant that I could still uphold quality curriculum, which, as you know, is a key principle in differentiation. Hence, I was confident, even at times when I was disorganised or rushing from one lesson to the next, that my lessons aligned with the relevant curriculum.

In the next section, I will be taking you through how to create quality learning objectives for what students should know, understand and be able to do for a lesson. I will discuss how unit planning can enhance this process and help you be more efficient with the time you have. As you move through these steps, let this serve as another reminder that you still need to utilise universal design for learning approaches as you design your lessons and units. Your classroom will have students with learning difficulties, disabilities and other needs that require reasonable adjustments according to the Disability Standards for Education 2005; hence, do not solely rely upon differentiation for these reasonable adjustments. You will be setting clear learning objectives for a given year level in this next section, and your aim will be to ensure that all students in your classroom can access these.

Setting clear learning objectives (KUDs)

The basis for any effective differentiation starts from knowing what you want your students to *Know, Understand and be able to Do* (known as KUDs). I will refer to learning objectives and KUDs interchangeably throughout the book. You will be drawing your KUDs from the curriculum framework your state or territory uses; however, I will be utilising the Version 9 Australian Curriculum for both unit and lesson planning, as it is most widely used in Australia. KUDs must be drawn from the curriculum, as the premise of differentiation is to uphold quality curriculum, to ensure learners are meaningfully engaged and focused on the essential knowledge, skills and understanding that the discipline values. You may already follow a particular structure with your learning objectives – for example, I see many teachers adopt *learning intentions and success criteria*. There is nothing wrong with continuing this method in your classroom. However, where teachers fall down with this method is when they try to create differentiated learning intentions and success criteria. In this attempt at differentiation, different students are subjected to different learning intentions and success criteria, with students with lower readiness given intentions and success criteria with lower expectations. This is not differentiation.

Holding high expectations of your students is crucial in a differentiated classroom (as represented in Figure 10), as it is these expectations that drive students to learn. Often, we see teachers *dumb down* (Dixon, 2005) the curriculum and learning objectives for students who perhaps have lower readiness or extensive needs. This dumbing down, in my professional opinion, is more often than not done out of care for the students, with the teacher wanting to make sure that their student sees some success through easier tasks.

We know, however, that this practice does not see students grow academically or be challenged in their learning (Graham, 2019). It only makes the knowledge gap wider and wider, with more students falling behind. When you hold high expectations for your students and aim to differentiate in a variety of ways, you can achieve a more inclusive education system for all students. A full disclaimer and a word of caution here – differentiation should not replace providing reasonable adjustments to students who need them, such as students with disability. Nor should differentiation mean you need to abandon other teaching methods and practices. There are times when you need to utilise explicit instruction, inquiry, project learning, etc.; however, differentiation can help facilitate these. Some of your students may require modifications to be made, and again, you do not and should not abandon these. Differentiation is a tier 1 practice, as outlined in Chapter 1, meaning that all students should be part of the differentiated classroom.

Figure 10: The relationship between quality curriculum and quality differentiation

High-quality curriculum  **High-quality differentiation**

Your first step is to start by opening the relevant curriculum framework you are working with. In this example, I will be using the Version 9 Australian Curriculum, focusing on Year 10 Science. You can access the Version 9 Australian curriculum here: https://v9.australiancurriculum.edu.au/. You will need to navigate to *Learning areas* and select the learning area and year level you wish to focus on. Here, in Figure 11, you can see I have selected Science and Year 10. Click the submit button. The Victorian Curriculum has a similar structure to the Version 9 Australian Curriculum, except that content descriptions are grouped into "strands" and "sub-strands", with the achievement standard named the same as in the Australian Curriculum. Similarly, the New South Wales Curriculum is organised in a slightly different way, with "outcomes" comparable to achievement standards, and "content" comparable to content descriptions. You may use these if you choose.

Figure 11: Screen to select subject and year level for V 9.0 curriculum

Having selected the year level and subject, you will be taken to a page that outlines two key aspects of the curriculum:

1. The achievement standards
2. The content descriptions.

The achievement standards describe the quality of learning typically expected of students throughout the year. You will notice that they begin with the statement "By the end of Year…", telling you that by the completion of that academic year students should have demonstrated each of the listed achievement standards. These are sequenced in a way that describes the student's progress in the learning area. You utilise these standards to make judgements about the quality of learning for a student, which is typically done through summative assessment. Assessment is covered in more detail in the following chapter.

The content descriptions specify what you, as the teacher, are expected to teach your students. These are well-researched and provide the scope and sequence of teaching in the various learning areas. Your role, as teacher, is to determine how to best cater for students' readiness, interests and preferences in order to be able to teach them the content, skills and understanding. You will be drawing upon both the achievement standards and content descriptions to create the KUDs.

Let's take the highlighted Year 10 Science achievement standard in Figure 12. What is fantastic about the Australian Curriculum website is that when you select the achievement standard that you want to focus on, it directly links you to the relevant content description. In this example, I selected "By the end of Year 10 students explain the processes that underpin heredity and genetic diversity and describe the evidence supporting the theory of evolution by natural selection".

Figure 12: Screen with highlighted achievement standard

Achievement standard: Year 10

By the end of Year 10 students explain the processes that underpin heredity and genetic diversity and describe the evidence supporting the theory of evolution by natural selection. They sequence key events in the origin and evolution of the universe and describe the supporting evidence for the big bang theory. They describe trends in patterns of global climate change and identify causal factors. They explain how Newton's laws describe motion and apply them to predict motion of objects in a system. They explain patterns and trends in the periodic table and predict the products of reactions and the effect of changing reactant and reaction conditions. Students analyse the importance of publication and peer review in the development of scientific knowledge and analyse the relationship between science, technologies and engineering. They analyse the key factors that influence interactions between science and society.

Students plan and conduct safe, valid and reproducible investigations to test relationships or develop explanatory models. They explain how they have addressed any ethical and intercultural considerations when generating or using primary and secondary data. They select equipment and use it efficiently to generate and record appropriate sample sizes and replicable data with precision. They select and construct effective representations to organise, process and summarise data and information. They analyse and connect a variety of data and information to identify and explain patterns, trends, relationships and anomalies. They evaluate the validity and reproducibility of methods, and the validity of conclusions and claims. They construct logical arguments based on analysis of a variety of evidence to support conclusions and evaluate claims. They select and use content, language and text features effectively to achieve their purpose when communicating their ideas, findings and arguments to diverse audiences.

In selecting this standard, shown in Figure 12, the following content descriptions, shown in Figure 13, were automatically highlighted, thus making it easier for you to connect content descriptions and achievement standards together.

Figure 13: Content descriptions highlighted

AC9S10U01	AC9S10U02
explain the role of meiosis and mitosis and the function of chromosomes, DNA and genes in heredity and predict patterns of Mendelian inheritance	use the theory of evolution by natural selection to explain past and present diversity and analyse the scientific evidence supporting the theory

As I only want to focus on one lesson, I am not going to utilise both of these, but will focus on AC9S10U02: "use the theory of evolution by natural selection to explain past and present diversity and analyse the scientific evidence supporting the theory". You now have the basis for your KUDs to be created as outlined in Figure 14. Complete Supporting Activity 1 (page 51), by selecting an achievement standard and content description for a desired lesson from the selected lesson – use my example as a guide. There is no rule with the number of content descriptions and achievement standards to be used; however, less is more when thinking about lesson planning. I will discuss this when you look at designing assessment.

Figure 14: My selected achievement standard(s) and content description(s)

Achievement standard(s) and content description(s)

AS: Students explain the processes that underpin heredity and genetic diversity and describe the evidence supporting the theory of evolution by natural selection.

CD: Use the theory of evolution by natural selection to explain past and present diversity and analyse the scientific evidence supporting the theory.

Crafting understand statements

Your goal now is to design your KUDs from the selected achievement standard(s) and content description(s), starting with the *understand*. These can be the most difficult to create and people tend to confuse them with *know*. You may also think of these as conceptual understanding that can be taught through a range of subjects – also known as *concepts*. For example, "relationships" can form part of the understand, as relationships can be seen in all subject areas. The relationship between addition and subtraction in mathematics, the relationship between plant and animal cells, the relationship between the water of the Murray River and agriculture in Australia – these are just some examples to highlight how "relationships" can form part of the understand as a concept.

The reason we look to the achievement standards for the understand is because thinking about what you want students to understand allows you to be more intentional about why you are teaching what you are teaching. The Australian Curriculum is presented as a sequence of learning over time, highlighting that students build on their conceptual understanding across the years and over a range of learning areas. The content and skills you teach students will help them unpack the concepts covered (Wiggins & McTighe, 2005). Concepts, or *big ideas*, can be transferred to a variety of areas and can be applicable to other topics, issues, problems, processes or debates.

The images below (Figure 15) highlight some further examples of how concepts can be taught to enhance student understanding, but can be taught through content and in a variety of areas. While we have subjects at school, these should not be siloed. In life after school, we do not say to ourselves "Today I am going to use mathematics for part of the day, and then I will engage in some writing, which is English". We use a range of skills and knowledge in a variety of ways throughout our day. Concept-based teaching means that you can teach students to transfer this understanding to a broader context and to the real world.

Figure 15: Examples of how concepts can be taught across learning areas

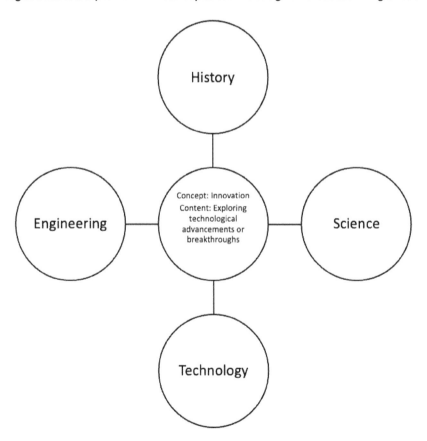

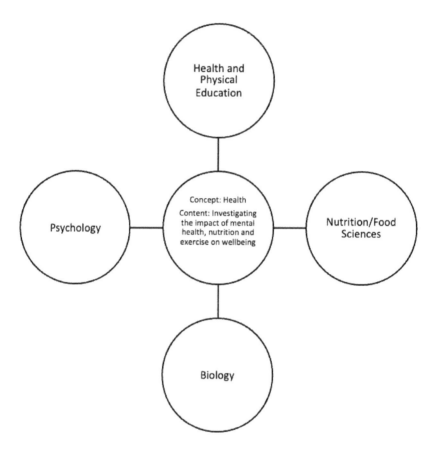

Here are some questions to consider when thinking about the understand and forming understand statements from Wiggins & McTighe (2005).

1. What are the "big ideas"?
2. What specific understandings about them are desired?
3. What misunderstandings are predictable?

You may want to explore this list of concepts from Simplicable: https://simplicable.com/thinking/concept.

Consider familiarising yourself with these (Figure 16), as this will help you to identify the understand when you start to delve into the achievement standards and content descriptions. This list is not exhaustive.

Figure 16: List of concepts

Adaptation	Freedom	Problem
Advancement	Friend	Product
Adventure	Future	Productivity
Algorithm	Game	Quality
Architecture	Government	Random
Art	Groupthink	Realism
Artificial Intelligence	Happiness	Reality
Assumptions	Humility	Resilience
Authenticity	Idealism	Rights
Automation	Imagination	Risk
Bravery	Improvisation	Rule
Business	Infinity	Safety
Cause	Influence	Sales
Change	Infrastructure	Sanity
Chaos	Insanity	Science
Civility	Intangible	Self-fulfillment
Communication	Intuition	Service
Competition	Joy	Society
Constraints	Justice	Software
Contract	Law	Sport
Control	Leadership	Stability
Coolness	Love	Story
Cuisine	Magic	Strategy
Culture	Management	Student
Dance	Marketing	Style
Design	Meaning	System
Development	Measurement	Talent
Difficult	Media	Tangible
Digital	Military	Teacher
Easy	Money	Technology
Economy	Motivation	Theory
Education	Music	Thought
Effect	Optimism	Time
Empathy	Past	Truth
Ethics	Pessimism	Universe
Experiment	Philosophy	Values
Fact	Play	Virtual
Failure	Pragmatic	Win
Fairness	Principles	Wonder
Family	Privacy	Work

Using the list above, select one of the concepts and complete Supporting Activity 2 (page 51) by filling in the diagram. Identify a concept and make it link to two or three learning areas. You could draw the content from the Australian Curriculum here too or your own mandated curriculum.

The understand can be found in both the achievement standard and the content descriptions; however, it is more likely to be in the achievement standard, because this highlights depth of understanding for a particular learning area. So, looking back at my Year 10 Science AS and CS, you can see through my underlining below (Figure 17), that there are quite a few concepts that can be used to create the understand. You do not need to cover all in one lesson. You may focus on the same understand for a period of time, depending on how your students are responding. I often say to teachers to think about understand as a garden shed – the understand goals are akin to the foundation and the structure of the shed and provide the shed with support for the shed's purpose.

Figure 17: Underlining concepts in the AS and CD

AS: Students explain the processes that underpin heredity and genetic diversity and describe the evidence supporting the theory of evolution by natural selection.

CD: Use the theory of evolution by natural selection to explain past and present diversity and analyse the scientific evidence supporting the theory.

Now that you have the conceptual basis for what your students will understand, you need to make understand statements. These take the format of: *Students will understand that...* Before you look at my examples, I want you to have a practice at writing three understand statements – one each for the concepts of *theory*, *process* and *past*. Write your answers in Supporting Activity 3 (page 52).

After completing your initial statements, compare your answers with mine below in Figure 18.

Figure 18: My example of understand *statements*

Tom's understand statements

- Students will understand that heredity and genetic diversity are determined by a series of actions.

- Students will understand that scientific theories are a way of explaining the world.
- Students will understand that the past has shaped the diversity in the world.

You can see that some of the elements of these statements are broad enough that they allow students to transfer knowledge across subject areas. As you begin to teach the knowledge and skills in the lesson or unit (which come from our *knows* and *do's*), this helps students to see the connection to the *understand* and the concept embedded within this statement. For example, I could show my students the steps of how certain genes are passed on to children from their parents, and how these children will pass their genes on to their children, all the while highlighting a *process* (concept) through a series of actions. Many will argue that an understand statement should be so broad that it can be applied to any subject – I disagree with this. I think you need to highlight the concept and really drill down into what that concept is. For example, *theories* are typically supported by evidence, and are used to make sense of a phenomenon. This is why I have highlighted that they are a way of explaining the world. Based on this new knowledge, revise your three *understand* statements by completing Supporting Activity 4 (page 52).

So, now you have your understand statements based on the selected achievement standard(s) and content description(s). My example is below in Figure 19.

Figure 19: My examples of understand *statements connected to curriculum*

Tom's example

Achievement standard(s) and content description(s)

AS: Students explain the processes that underpin heredity and genetic diversity and describe the evidence supporting the theory of evolution by natural selection.

CD: Use the theory of evolution by natural selection to explain past and present diversity and analyse the scientific evidence supporting the theory.

Students will understand that:
- Heredity and genetic diversity are determined by a series of actions.
- Scientific theories are a way of explaining the world.
- The past has shaped the diversity in the world.

Crafting the *know* and *do* statements

The next step is to look at what you want students to know and do, after forming the understand statement(s). These components are drawn from the content descriptions, and are taught to students so they can achieve the big ideas (or the understand). Using the content descriptions, you need to ask yourself, "What knowledge do I want students to acquire?" According to Wiggins and McTighe (2005), knowledge is often in the form of:

- Key vocabulary
- Terminology
- Definitions
- Key factual information
- Formulas
- Critical details
- Important events and people
- Sequence and timelines.

An even simpler way to look for the know is by looking for the nouns and adjectives in the content descriptions (if using the Australian Curriculum). A question to ask yourself is, "What am I asking students to learn?" It is important to be specific here. For example, simply stating that "students will know key vocabulary" does not really provide clear guidance on what the vocabulary is. Similarly, listing the vocabulary itself (for example, "Students will know what symbiotic, mutualism, commensalism and parasitism is") does not tell a student much either. However, if you were to say "Students will know types of relationships plants and animals have with one another and how they affect their relationships", you still need to teach key vocabulary for them to understand the similarities and differences between them. *Know* statements are typically written as "Students will know that..."

The *do's*, on the other hand, are the skills you are asking your students to acquire as a result of participating in this lesson or unit. You can draw the *do's* from the verbs in the content descriptions. It may help you to highlight the verbs before creating your do statements. I find that these are usually the easiest to create, as the verb in the content description can guide you. Bloom's taxonomy, which highlights verbs in a hierarchical order, provides you with a list of the common verbs of things you ask students to do (see Figure 20). *Do* statements are typically written as "Students will be able to..."

Figure 20: Bloom's taxonomy

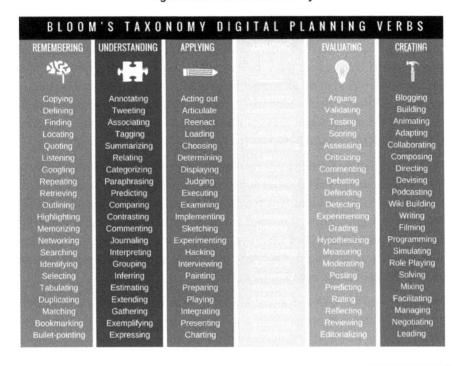

SOURCE: HEICK (2021).

Using the below content description, pull out the key *knows* and *do's* and complete Supporting Activity 5 (page 53). Then look at my example in Figure 21 and compare.

CD: Use the theory of evolution by natural selection to explain past and present diversity and analyse the scientific evidence supporting the theory.

Figure 21: My **knows** *and* **do's**

Tom's example

Students will know:

- How the theory of natural selection can explain evolution
- How natural selection contributes to diversity in populations.

Students will be able to:

- Use scientific theories
- Explain the impact of the past and present on diversity
- Analyse scientific evidence.

Congratulations! You have now identified, using quality curriculum, what you want students to know, understand and be able to do for a selected lesson. This forms the basis for your lesson(s) or unit. It is at this point that I make an executive decision and determine whether these learning objectives can cover more than one lesson. If you are asking your students to know and be able to do all these things in 45 minutes, you may be asking too much of them. I know that when I was teaching at one school I could have easily taught this in one lesson; however, in another school I worked at, I know that this would have taken a few lessons.

What we are saying here is that, no matter who is in your classroom, every student is going to work towards achieving these KUD goals in one form or another. Now, I know what you are thinking: you may have some students who have a significantly modified curriculum or require substantial-to-extensive adjustments, all of which you will still need to do, while providing a differentiated classroom. Our first priority is to try our best to get all students to meet these learning objectives.

I established earlier that the understand is the shed; however, the knowledge and skills are the various gardening tools, pots, seeds and equipment, and each item serves a specific function within the shed and serves the purpose of the understand. Below, in Figure 22, are the final KUD goals based on my selected subject at Year 10 Science.

Figure 22: My final learning objectives

Tom's final learning objectives

Achievement standard(s) and content descriptions

AS: Students explain the processes that underpin heredity and genetic diversity and describe the evidence supporting the theory of evolution by natural selection.

CD: Use the theory of evolution by natural selection to explain past and present diversity and analyse the scientific evidence supporting the theory.

Students will understand that:
- Heredity and genetic diversity are determined by a series of actions.
- Scientific theories are a way of explaining the world.
- The past has shaped the diversity in the world.

Students will know:
- How the theory of natural selection can explain evolution
- How natural selection contributes to diversity in populations.

Students will be able to:
- Use scientific theories
- Explain the impact of the past and present on diversity
- Analyse scientific evidence.

Evaluating and refining learning objectives

I am a firm believer that, in order to develop effective learning objectives, you need to see examples of poorly written objectives to understand why they would not be effective in the classroom. Let's explore an example of poorly designed learning objectives. I want to reassure you that designing clear and relevant learning objectives takes time and practice. You won't get it right from the get-go. When I looked back at my learning objectives when I first started teaching, I was horrified to see that they truly did not connect with the curriculum I was teaching – I don't even know what I had based them on, and I made so many assumptions! The learning objectives in Figure 23 were designed from the Version 9 Australian Curriculum for Year 7 Health and Physical Education for one lesson of approximately an hour and a half.

Figure 23: Example of poorly designed learning objectives

Achievement standard(s) and content descriptions

AS: Students will apply and transfer movement skills and movement concepts across situations. They implement and evaluate the effectiveness of movement strategies on movement outcomes. They select, use and refine strategies to support inclusion, fair play and collaboration across a range of movement contexts.

CD: Investigate modifications to equipment, rules and scoring systems that support fair play and inclusive participation.

Students will understand that:
- They can use different equipment in different ways.
- They can apply the skills they have learned and transfer them to other learning experiences.

Students will know:
- How different equipment to hit the ball into the correct position is executed
- How to connect what they have learned in this lesson and apply it to a game situation.

Students will be able to:

- Apply the tactical concepts of hitting a forehand and backhand stroke
- Create a rally game-like situation
- Apply their understanding by completing the exit card.

Take the time to review the above learning objectives and outline areas of strength and areas for concern, based on what you have learned should make up good learning objectives. Complete Supporting Activity 6 (page 53), which asks you to identify areas of strength in the above learning objectives and areas of concern. Once you have completed this activity, compare your answers with mine below in Figure 24.

Figure 24: Analysis of learning objectives

Strengths	Areas of concern
It was evident that the teacher tried to make their *understand* broad.	• What students will be able to do was not drawn from the content description. Students needed to be able to *investigate*.
	• The understand was not based on big ideas or concepts and was more geared towards *know*.
	• The know did not really connect with the content or what the content description was asking.
	• There was much overlap between the three learning objectives.

So now you have been stepped through how to create effective learning objectives, and you have seen an example of poorly designed learning objectives and why they are not effective. It is now your turn to practise this part of the dance of differentiation! In Supporting Activity 7 (page 54), I have provided you with another achievement standard and relevant content description, taken from the Version 9 Australian Curriculum for Year 2 Mathematics. Create your learning objectives based on what I have provided you with.

Lastly, you will select your own achievement standard and content description from your chosen area, creating your own learning objectives in Supporting Activity 8 (page 55).

Learning objectives for unit planning

Just as you have done above for your lesson, you can be even more proactive with your planning and create the learning objectives for your whole unit – doing so with other faculty members or colleagues. You can then have the learning objectives set as a group and select the relevant ones for each lesson. In fact, creating learning objectives with other faculty members promotes collaboration, encouraging them to adopt this approach in their teaching too, meaning that you can have a wider effect on teachers. Creating your learning objectives for a unit of work highlights the sequence of learning and logical progression of content and skills that need to be acquired, while teaching concepts. In later chapters, we will look at ways you can collaborate with your colleagues for differentiation.

Chapter summary and reflection

In this chapter, we have examined the beginning steps of the backwards by design approach. Here, you engaged in how to create quality learning objectives, also known as KUDs, as the starting point for differentiation. You have seen that all students in your inclusive classrooms will work towards these learning objectives. Each step for creating the learning objective has been outlined, and you have had practice in creating learning objectives for a variety of different learning areas. Take a moment now to reflect on your learning so far. Think about how you have applied learning goals or objectives in your classroom. *Was this similar to the way learning objectives are constructed in this chapter? Are they different?*

1. **Describe.** What were your key learnings from this chapter?

_____

_____

_____

_____

_____

_____

_____

2. **Interpret.** What does this experience mean for you, as you embark upon this dance of differentiation?

_____

_____

_____

_____

_____

_____

3. **Evaluate.** How valuable was this learning experience?

_____

_____

_____

_____

_____

4. **Plan.** How will you apply your learning?

_____

_____

_____

_____

_____

_____

Supporting Activity 1

Achievement standards and content descriptions

AS:

CD:

Supporting Activity 2

Linking concepts to learning areas

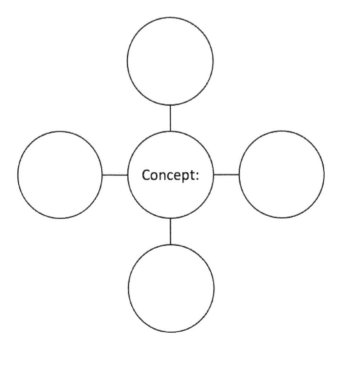

Supporting Activity 3

My initial *understand* statements

Supporting Activity 4

My revised *understand* statements

Supporting Activity 5

Know and *do* statements

CD: Use the theory of evolution by natural selection to explain past and present diversity and analyse the scientific evidence supporting the theory.

Students will know...

Students will be able to...

Supporting Activity 6

Areas of strength and concern in the established learning objectives

Strengths	Areas of concern

Supporting Activity 7

Creation of learning objectives for Year 2 Mathematics

Achievement standard(s) and content descriptions:

AS: They use uniform informal units to measure and compare shapes and objects.

CD: Measure and compare objects based on length, capacity and mass using appropriate uniform informal units and smaller units for accuracy when necessary.

Students will understand that:

Students will know:

Students will be able to:

Supporting Activity 8

Creation of your own learning objectives

Achievement standard(s) and content descriptions:

AS:

CD:

Students will understand that:

Students will know:

Students will be able to:

CHAPTER 3

Assessment as the opening move

"The first step is the hardest - making a bold move, especially in dance, sets the tone for the entire performance."

- ANONYMOUS

Learning objectives

By the end of this chapter:

- Teachers will understand that assessment contributes to the proactive and responsive nature of differentiation.
- Teachers will know that assessment informs differentiation decisions, meaning well-designed assessment tools are imperative in knowing one's students.
- Teachers will be able to design differentiated assessments based on equity.
- Teachers will be able to design appropriate assessment methods that support learning objectives.

Figure 25: Backwards by design

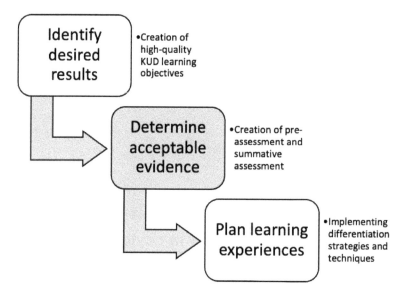

Continuing from your work in utilising understanding by design (Wiggins & McTighe, 2005, 2011) to create your learning objectives, or KUDs, the aim now is to consider the assessment evidence needed to determine what your students already know, understand and can do, in relation to the learning objectives. Some students will have more knowledge, skills and understanding than others and this is why we employ differentiation. Furthermore, the aim is to determine what ongoing assessment methods will need to be employed for effective differentiation, to ensure you know where your students are at. Similarly, you need to consider how you will design summative assessment tasks that are differentiated, so students can demonstrate their learning at the end of a unit of work in a manner that allows them to show what they know in the best way possible.

The use of assessment is a cyclical process and is something that may or may not be familiar to you already. Many of you reading this book may be used to providing one form of assessment – usually summative assessment – at the end of a unit of work, which you report on to parents/caregivers. You may not be used to embedding different types of assessments at different times throughout a unit of work, so I ask you to keep an open mind on how you might adapt what you currently do, to incorporate more assessment types into your teaching. I also want to preface this chapter by saying that I have not provided you with every way that you can utilise the different assessment types for differentiation, but I have outlined some of the ways I have found success.

As established in Chapter 1, assessment informs differentiation decisions, and you use assessment to gather data on your students. Typically, you use assessment to determine students' strengths and areas for concern, to make judgements about students' academic performance, to guide flexible grouping strategies, to develop instructional plans, and to lead and manage a classroom (Tomlinson & Moon, 2013). Obtaining data to inform your differentiation decisions is a cyclical process – you do not just assess students once and base your decisions on this. It needs to be ongoing. As outlined in Figure 26, you will collect data from your students – this data will come in all shapes and forms, depending on the way you choose to differentiate. For example, if I were wanting to differentiate by students' interests, I would be assessing to determine what my students' interests were at that time. Conversely, if I were determining students' readiness for a particular topic, then I might be asking them questions about what they know, understand and can do. When you have collected data from your assessments, you use this data to inform your differentiation decisions and how you might structure lessons. Again, the assessment does not end here – you reflect on how well your students have done and collect data on their progress again. In my case, I assessed, in some form or another, after each lesson. Some of my assessments were quick and easy, and others were more intricate. We will explore these in this chapter. The most important thing to note about assessment is that it assists you as teacher to determine what students currently know, what they need to know, and what they need to know next. This informs the learning opportunities you provide to those students.

Figure 26: Cyclical process of data collection

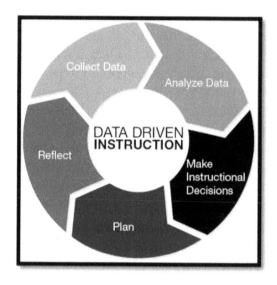

Types of assessment

There are three types of assessment you can use to determine what your students know, understand and are able to do.

1. **Assessment for learning (known as pre-assessment)** is typically gathered from a range of sources and is used to inform future teaching; hence, it is usually completed before teaching. Teachers adapt what they teach and how they teach in response to data collected. For example, you may have taken your students through a lesson on the environment, asking students to know what bushfires, floods, droughts or cyclones are, as well as their consequences. You may find, however, that after this lesson students are still struggling to understand this. Therefore, you may need to adapt and spend another lesson working through this content. Pre-assessment is crucial, as this informs student placement in the lesson, allowing you to take a proactive approach. For example, flexible grouping may be employed, with pre-assessment used to determine which groups students are placed into. There has

been much research, however, that shows that teachers struggle to implement assessment for learning (Mills et al., 2014; Westbroek et al., 2020).

2. **Assessment as learning (known as formative assessment)** is typically given throughout a unit of work, providing students with an opportunity for learning at the same time as assessment, and is usually integrated into the act of teaching. Teachers provide feedback to students during learning, to support and develop their metacognitive skills and enable them to become "better" learners. You use formative assessment to help students develop their capacity for self-evaluation. Formative assessment is low stakes in that it informs day-to-day decisions and allows you to take a responsive approach to differentiation.

3. **Assessment of learning (known as summative assessment)** is where students demonstrate what they know, understand and can do, and is typically completed at the conclusion of a unit of work. Summative assessment can be formal or informal and is often linked to specific criteria. In the case of the Australian Curriculum, summative assessments are designed so students can demonstrate what they know, understand and can do in relation to the achievement standards. You typically apply a grading scale to summative assessments, reporting progress to parents.

If you put these assessment types into the context of dance, it may help you to conceptualise how each of these work in tandem with one another. Let's imagine that you have decided to learn the tango. You might start by watching some videos on YouTube to visualise the steps. Here you might find that the tango has some similarities to other types of dances you already know. Using the video has helped solidify what you already know and don't yet know and has acted as a pre-assessment. You might start practising the dance in front of the mirror – over and over again –and revisiting other dance videos. As you watch yourself dance and compare this to the videos on YouTube, you might adapt the way you tango. This can be likened to formative assessment. Lastly, you might decide to enrol in a dance competition, where the judges will award you with a prize, depending on how well you execute the tango. This may be likened to summative assessment. You can utilise each of these throughout a unit of work, as shown in Figure 27. I want to encourage you to move beyond just *pen and paper* for assessment, understanding that almost anything students do or say can be used as assessment.

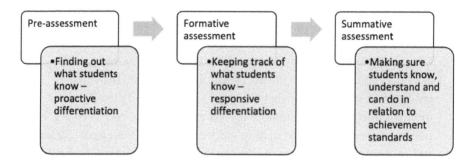

Figure 27: Utilising pre-assessment, formative assessment and summative assessment

Pre-assessment

As you progress through this section of the chapter, you need to make a decision as to how you will differentiate – remembering from the Introduction that you can choose to differentiate by readiness, interests or learner preferences, according to content, process or product. My advice here is to focus on one element of differentiation and do it well, rather than trying to differentiate in too many ways at once – for example, trying to differentiate content and process according to learner preferences and readiness. The reason you need to make this decision now is because this determines what you will pre-assess for in your lesson. There is a common hesitation to pre-assess students, as many teachers feel that this detracts from the already precious lesson time (Roberts & Inman, 2023), but it can actually save you time, particularly when it comes to curriculum compacting, discussed in the next chapter. Again, you might need to lean into the uncomfortable and be willing to abandon some of your existing pedagogies or ways of teaching. This is ok!

Preparing assessment for differentiation by readiness

Our classrooms are diverse, and some students come to our classrooms with more knowledge and understanding in certain areas compared to others. We also know that this is not fixed – that the "C grade" students are not always going to be "C grade" in everything. This may require a change in thinking for you – moving beyond thinking that your students with lower grades are of lower readiness. A clear example was me when I was in school – I was a "straight A" student in all subjects, except for mathematics – I just could not wrap my head around the procedural nature of mathematics and would often receive a C. That being said, when it came to the topic of measurement, I was quite adept in this area, receiving A and B grades. I had different readiness levels, not just in subjects, but in topics. This will be the same for your students. This is crucial to remember and can really help you to create a differentiated classroom that recognises student growth, instead of saying that student growth is fixed within students' capabilities.

You might be thinking, "So how do I determine the readiness of my students?" This is where ongoing pre- and post-assessment really can enhance your differentiation. If you just assume student readiness without any evidence, then I would argue that you are not differentiating at all. However, creating small activities or assessments that help determine readiness in a more concrete way and using this evidence to make decisions in your lesson – that's differentiation!

The next stage is to use the learning objectives to create your assessment task that will help you collect evidence on student readiness. These assessment tasks, often known as pre-assessment, are usually completed at the end of the previous lesson, to help inform your next lesson's decisions.

There is one pertinent point that needs to be made here. You must assess the knowledge, understandings and skills identified through the learning objectives (Tomlinson & Moon, 2013). Where people fall short is that they might assess students on one *know* and that's all, forgetting to assess the skills and what students should understand. This does not tell you much about what the student can do or understand. The only proviso here is that if you were planning to spend a few lessons on the same learning objectives, then you might assess part of the learning objectives at certain points in time.

Personally, I have always been a fan of the exit card – something that takes 5 minutes to administer and collect, giving me great insight into my students in relation to the learning objectives. You can get quite creative with them too, moving away from traditional pen and paper and from just question and answer. I have had students draw things, make diagrams, fill in graphic organisers, and even do small TikTok-style videos linking to the KUDs.

Before you look at my examples of pre-assessments, I want you to look back at the learning objectives established in Chapter 2. Here I will give you some choice. You could focus on the learning objectives I designed, or on the objectives you designed. Outline two or three questions you could ask your students in relation to the selected learning objectives to determine how ready they are to learn the KUDs for the next lesson. Write your answers in Supporting Activity 1 (page 82). My advice is to not overcomplicate it, as the more you ask of your students, the more confused you can become in determining their readiness. After you have completed the activity, look at my example questions below in Figure 28.

Figure 28: Tom's example of pre-assessment for readiness

Pre-assessment

1. Provide an example that illustrates how natural selection acts to shape genetic diversity within a population.
2. How did the theory of natural selection come about, and how does it connect with evolution?

You can see that, while I have only two questions, these assess all elements of my learning objectives. By having students use an example, they will need to explain how that animal or plant has changed over time (past and present were what students needed to *understand*), outline what natural selection is, and connect this theory with evolution. While I have not directly provided scientific evidence to analyse, I want to see if my students can draw upon knowledge from previous years.

Let's look at an example of a pre-assessment and a set of learning objectives from Year 7 Geography in Figure 29. (Disclaimer: the KUDs themselves are not well designed.) Critically examine the pre-assessment against the learning objectives and outline the strengths and areas for concern in Supporting Activity 2 (page 82).

Figure 29: Year 7 Geography learning objectives

Students will understand that:

- The location and distribution of water resources in Australia, their implication, and strategies to manage the sustainability of water.
- The location and distribution of services and facilities, and implication for liveability of place.

Students will know:

- How to identify and locate some of Australia's major water sources (ground water and surface water)
- How to explain factors that contribute to variability in water resources
- How to examine the strategy adopted to manage the sustainability of resources
- How to analyse the distribution of facilities in urban and rural areas and how they affect the lives of people in the areas.

Students will be able to:
- Locate the distribution of water resources in Australia
- Prepare strategies to manage the sustainability of water
- Prepare the liveability index and draw the conclusion between availability of resources and people.

Pre-assessment

1. What is Australia's most major source of water?
2. How can we reduce water consumption in our households?

As you can likely see, the pre-assessment does not fully align with the learning objectives. In fact, this highlights that what the teacher was asking of their students was too much for one lesson, which is why I stress the importance of not creating too many KUDs for one lesson. The first question, while designed to link to Australia's distribution of water, is also worded quite vaguely, and may be confusing for some students. Lastly, students were not able to demonstrate what they were able to do in relation to the learning objectives. The teacher could have been creative with how they assessed here. For example, students could have been given a map of Australia and asked to colour in the areas on the map where they thought Australia's water supply was located. Similarly, students could have been asked to create a plan with a list of strategies for households to become more sustainable. These are just two examples of many.

You can see, however, that when we administer pre-assessments, they tell us a lot about what students know, understand and are able to do. You do not have to assess each of the KUDs in every pre-assessment you administer, as long as you are assessing each of them at some point in the unit. However, most of the time it makes sense to gauge all three, given that your lesson KUDs may change quite dramatically over the course of a unit. Take the two examples of pre-assessments below in Figure 30. These two "exit tickets" were administered to my Year 12 Business Innovation students at the completion of a lesson, to guide my decisions for the next lesson. I was starting a new unit of work and I wanted to determine students' previous knowledge of "value proposition", as I knew this had been covered in the Year 11 course. Furthermore, I wanted to find out more about students' understanding of how value proposition fits into the bigger scheme of things, linking value proposition to business success and how businesses can cycle between success and failure. These two students had very different readiness levels, with one student recalling the three elements of value proposition, and the other student showing a greater connection between value proposition and what this means for businesses. Hence, they informed the way I approached my lesson and what my students were doing, depending on their readiness. I will discuss this more in the next chapter.

Figure 30: Examples of exit tickets for pre-assessment

Student 1

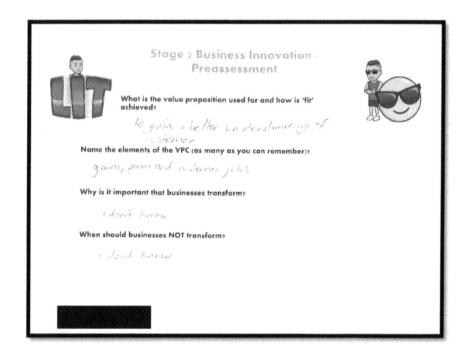

Student 2

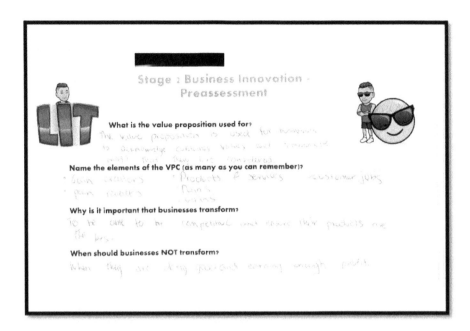

In contrast, I used to teach Year 9 Literacy and I knew that I needed to explore irony and the role of irony in written and spoken texts in the next lesson I taught them. This was an incredibly small class, only around seven students, so I often moved away from exit tickets to classroom discussions as pre-assessments. We made the rule early on that whenever we had discussions, everyone would need to contribute and there would be no hiding. So, rather than the exit ticket, I asked students to look at the images on the board (shown below in Figure 31) and to each take turns outlining what they thought these images represented. I was able to gauge what they knew about irony from these discussions. To my surprise, though, all of my students struggled to relate these pictures to irony. This told me that exploring irony needed to be more explicit in my next lesson and that, perhaps, providing a range of written, spoken and visual media that highlighted irony was where we needed to go as a class.

Figure 31: Class discussion prompt to determine student readiness

Now it is your turn. Either using the learning objectives you created in Chapter 1 or after creating new learning objectives (which is great practice), design a pre-assessment to gauge student readiness against those learning objectives and complete Supporting Activity 3 (page 83). It is important to note that you will explore what to do with the results and data from these pre-assessments when you start looking at tiering in the next chapter.

One of my favourite ways to pre-assess students, particularly when I want to know more about what they can *do*, is using graphic organisers. Graphic organisers can link incredibly well to the verbs – or the doing words – in the content descriptions. For example, in Year 3 Mathematics, one of the content descriptors is "to make, compare and classify objects, identifying key features and explaining why these features make them suited to their uses". If I want to pre-assess my students on their readiness to compare and classify objects, I could get them to complete a double bubble graphic organiser (shown in Figure 32), which is designed to assist students to compare and classify. This is just a different way of getting them to show me what they know in relation to my learning objectives, beyond just question and answer.

Figure 32: Double bubble graphic organiser

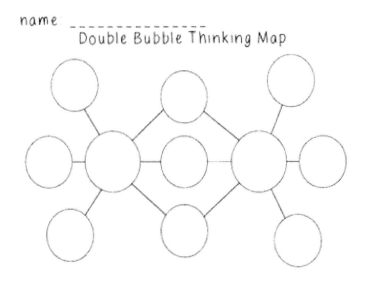

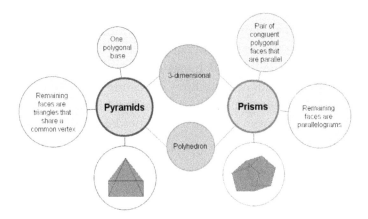

Comparing enhances meaning

SOURCE: HTTPS://WIKI.WESTMINSTERPUBLICSCHOOLS.ORG.

Some common graphic organisers and their connection to verbs are shown in Figure 33.

Figure 33: Graphic organiser comparison to verbs

Graphic organiser	Connection to verbs
Circle map	To explain and define
Spider map	To describe
Venn diagram	Explain, compare, contrast
Flow chart	Sequence, order
Bubble map	Describe
Double bubble map	Compare, contrast, classify
Tree map	Categorising, classifying
Multiflow map	Analyse
Brace map	Identify
Freyer diagram	Define, describe

Finally, I have included below (Figure 34) some further examples of ways that you can pre-assess your students. This is by no means an exhaustive list. Many of them you likely do already, and some of them you may not be familiar with. Later in the book I discuss the importance of developing confidence in differentiation, so for now, select one of the strategies below and start to plan out how you might use this in your subject. Supporting Activity 4 (page 83) gives you space to write your ideas.

Figure 34: Examples of pre-assessment strategies

Name of strategy	How it could be implemented
Hand signals	You can ask students to hold up fingers depending on how confident they are with specific knowledge or understanding, from holding up 5 for most confident to no fingers indicating no confidence. Many will argue that this is very much for primary students, but my secondary students really got into this after a while. Alternatively, ask students for 3–2–1 (3 being most confident and no fingers being least confident).
KWL (know, want to know, and have learned)	Students can be asked, either in groups or individually, what they know about a topic, what they want to know, and what they have learned. Completing this individually allows you to gain a deeper understanding on a student level. This is harder to gauge when implemented in groups or as a whole class. This could be completed verbally or written down.
Quizzes	Individual quizzes can be effective at gauging student readiness; however, depending on the format, they may not be as accurate. For example, Kahoot!, while engaging, puts time pressure on students, meaning they are more likely to select any answer due to the competition. Hence, this may not reflect their actual readiness levels.
Internet surveys	I utilised these a lot. I would often create Microsoft Forms and embed these into my school's learning management system. I developed a bank of questions that I would then drag and drop into a Microsoft Form. You could use Google Forms too. I found these quicker and easier than pen and paper, and there is no need to collect and store the written versions.
Observations and conversations	Once I became confident in differentiation, I started to allow my students more independence and self-direction. The payoff was that I had more time to spend with students individually. Conversations are incredibly powerful for gauging readiness, interests and learner preferences. Similarly, observing students as they undertook activities allowed me to adapt within the lesson.
Exit or entry tickets	Much like internet quizzes, but in *pen and paper* form. These are my go-to. Again, you can use these to assess readiness, interests and learner preferences. Administer these at the end of a lesson to guide you for the following lesson.

Name of strategy	How it could be implemented
Mini whiteboards	My students loved these, although I had to have some parameters for their use. We would do in-class quizzes, and I would ask students to hold up their answers using the mini whiteboards. I could quickly gauge their understanding with this. You can ask students to draw their answers too.
Self-ratings	Have students self-rate how they feel they are grasping a particular concept, knowledge or skill throughout the lesson or unit. You may use this as a guide for readiness, but consider another method to supplement. Readiness and confidence are not always the same.
Portfolios	In many of my classes, I would set portfolio work, having students collate all of their activities and work into a folder, or more recently, into online formats such as Microsoft OneNote. I could go into each student's portfolio throughout the unit and provide them with feedback, suggesting more appropriate activities depending on their readiness level and how this changed throughout the unit.

Preparing assessment for differentiation by interest

While gathering evidence on what students can know, understand and do is important in creating lessons based on readiness, you may also want to determine what your students' interests are at a certain point in time, to utilise these to increase student engagement. Attending to students' interests can help to maximise student learning (Tomlinson & Moon, 2013).

I have found that sometimes it can be challenging to connect students' interests to certain subjects and content areas. For example, when I taught Year 11 Nutrition, I had a group of students who had significant interest in Pokémon. There were times when I could connect Pokémon to certain aspects, such as designing a meal plan for Ash Ketchum (a Pokémon trainer), who leads an active lifestyle catching Pokémon all day; however, it was not always possible. Therefore, I would often use one of the earlier pre-assessments, such as an exit ticket, to ask students about their interests, but get them to connect the interest to the subject.

Utilising students' interests does not mean that you have to make it a free-for-all – whereby you assess for students interests broadly and include them in every lesson of every day. You may have a particular unit of work you want to cover and provide some choices to students, gauging which topics interest them the most out of the choices, helping you to narrow your approach. Take this example of an exit ticket I created for Year 11 Nutrition on health promotion, as shown below in Figure 35. This approach meant I could tally up the most popular topics in order to implement them in my lessons.

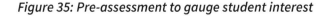

Figure 35: Pre-assessment to gauge student interest

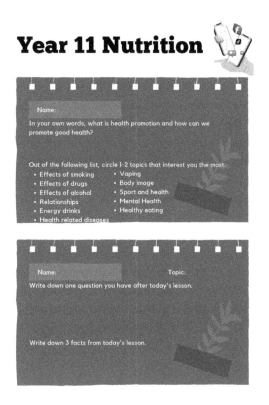

It is important to note that students' interests are always changing, so determining their interests regularly will help you to utilise their more current interests, harnessing engagement. Use the space in Supporting Activity 5 (page 84), to design a pre-assessment that gauges students' interest in your class. For those of you reading this book with perceived low readiness, keep the pre-assessment broad, gauging a range of interests. For those of you who feel you have some understanding of how to create pre-assessments for interests and therefore more readiness, select an area of focus for your subject, and create a pre-assessment that narrows the interests to your topic (as I have done with my health promotion topic). Lastly, those of you who are high readiness, create a pre-assessment that determines students' interests as well as readiness. Should you select this approach, you will need to utilise learning objectives too.

Preparing assessment for differentiation by learner preferences

"Learner preferences" is a relatively new term coined by Tomlinson (2022) and replaces her previous term "learner profiles" (Tomlinson, 2014). Learner preferences is very different from learning styles – which have become engrained in education terminology. In fact, when I conducted my research on teacher knowledge of differentiation, a significant number of my teacher participants referenced catering to learning styles. While not bad, as many older-generation teachers were taught about learning styles, this may shock many of you, but there is significant research that highlights that learning styles are a myth, and in fact the theory has been debunked. Psychologists Reiner and Willingham (2010, p. 36) stated: "Students may have preferences about how to learn, but no evidence suggests that catering to those preferences will lead to better learning." Learning styles were considered quite fixed in that, if you were a *visual learner*, this suggested you could only learn through visual means and any other way was not effective. In contrast, the term learner preferences recognises that students have different ways they prefer to learn and to demonstrate what they have learned. It is for this reason that differentiation by product (or output) – having students demonstrate what they know according to their learner preferences – can be really effective.

Using the space in Supporting Activity 6 (page 84), write down as many learner preferences as you can think of. Consider your own students: what are their preferred modes of learning and how do they enjoy demonstrating what they know? Much like students' interests, you can gauge students' learner preferences quite broadly or narrow these down to specific preferences you may want to utilise. Narrowing, however, cannot come at the expense of students not having a preference for learning. As Tomlinson (2022) outlined, learning preferences are fluid and they change with time, context and circumstances. Therefore, pre-assessing on a regular basis will help you to keep track of students' changing preferences.

In my experience, students are not always aware of their preferences in learning. This is particularly so if they have not been exposed to different ways of learning or demonstrating their learning. For example, a student may enjoy demonstrating their learning through a video presentation, but if not exposed, may not understand how this format works. Therefore, you may want to consider modelling some of these formats throughout your unit or lessons. I intentionally incorporated a range of ways of learning early on in my units of work, to expose students to these different options. For example, I would often use Microsoft Flip and have students record their answers through a TikTok-style approach – getting them used to the idea of demonstrating learning through videos. Similarly, I would print off blank storyboards and have students draw their answers through a story. This meant that, by the time the summative assessment came along at the end of the unit, I could provide students with a range of options for demonstrating their learning, and they were familiar with the learning preferences provided.

Formative assessment

Up until now, you have looked at designing pre-assessments to determine student readiness, interests and learner preferences, allowing you to be proactive in planning for differentiation, further informing differentiation decisions. Using formative assessments allows you to take more of a responsive approach to differentiation. Formative assessment does not just occur at one point in time and does not mean that you need to stop instruction to administer an assessment. In fact, Tomlinson (2022) argues that nearly all students' work can be assessed formally. What I love most about formative assessment is that you do not always have to be the judge of where students are at in their learning – you can allow students to become their own assessors, asking them to reflect on what they know, understand and can do.

Hattie (2003) outlines three questions to ask oneself when implementing formative assessment:

1. What is to be learned?
2. How is the learning progressing?
3. What will be learned next?

One of the ways I like students to track their own progress is through the use of checklists. I would implement these throughout a unit of work, collating them to determine whether I needed to provide some explicit instruction in certain areas. Similarly, like the example in Figure 36, I would have students complete the checklist before summative assessments – again, to help guide my future teaching. I asked students to not only tell me if they knew it or not, but to outline their confidence. In many instances, I could see commonalities between students, and chances were that if one student did not know or understand something, then many others did not either. Again, this meant I either needed to provide explicit instruction in that area or – achievement standards permitting – I would not incorporate it into the summative assessment. Similarly, when students ranked themselves as not confident in certain areas, I would employ other types of formative assessment to determine their readiness, rather than just relying on confidence as a measure of readiness.

Figure 36: Student checklist example

STAGE 1 NUTRITION

Topic 1: Micronutrients

Test Revision Checklist

	☺	?	!!
Which vitamins are water soluble and which are fat soluble and the differences between the two			
Factors that reduce absorption of calcium			
Functions of each of the vitamins			
Foods that contain high levels of Vitamin D			
Possible vitamin deficiencies for vegans			
What minerals and vitamins could someone with osteoporosis be deficient in and what sources could this come from			
Deficiencies in vitamin A, B, C, D, E & K and what conditions arise from this			
Food sources for all vitamins			
Functions of all vitamins and minerals			
Which vitamins are antioxidants and the effects of these			
Understand storage of vitamins and minerals			
Understand nutritional requirements of pregnant women and why they need certain micronutrients			
Effects of sodium on health			
Understand the difference between non-haem iron and haem iron			
Understand how some vitamins can play an active role in mineral absorption e.g. vitamin C increases iron uptake			
Result of deficiencies in minerals and what conditions arise from this			
Cooking methods and the effects this has on vitamins			
Functions of minerals			
RDI of adults and teenagers for calcium and the reason for the difference			
Effect that fibre can have on minerals and vitamins			
Explain the benefits of fortified foods			
Practical skills			
• Creation of a hypothesis			
• Recognising independent and dependant variables			
• Factors kept constant			
• How reliability is improved in a study			
• Understanding of how nutrition tables should be set out			
• Sample size			
• Repetition			
• Random and systematic errors			

For Tomlinson (2014), one of the ways that you can differentiate is through a learning menu, which we will explore in more depth in the next chapter. In essence, a learning menu allowed my students to take ownership in their learning, making decisions about what they wanted to learn and when they wanted to learn it. I would often employ learning menus as formative assessment, rather than as a graded portfolio of work. As a way of finding out how learning was progressing, I implemented an individual check-in system for each of the lessons, as shown below in Figure 37. I would ask them to bring their folio with them and to talk to me about what they had completed, what they had learned, and anything they were unsure about. This allowed me to guide them into tasks that might have assisted their learning or challenged them more. I used the formative assessment to guide students to tasks and learning that I thought would put them into their zone of proximal development, if they were not there already. Often, I saw common misconceptions arise, so I would address these as a class towards the end of the week.

Figure 37: Check-in system for portfolio

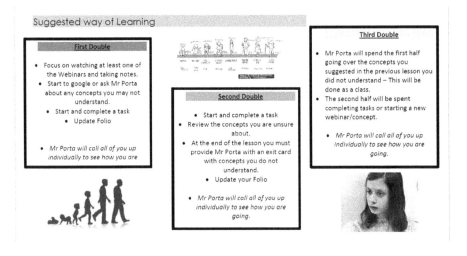

The point that I endeavour to make here is that formative assessment does not, and should not, be onerous for the student or the teacher. You should be looking back at the learning objectives for the lesson or unit, and determining if students are progressing towards these, through the formative assessment. Using the space in Supporting Activity 7 (page 84), reflect on your present use of formative assessment – how have you been utilising formative assessment? How might you use formative assessment more effectively? Where will you start?

Summative assessment

Summative assessment, as established, is more formal and "official" compared to formative assessment and pre-assessment (Tomlinson & Moon, 2013). This is because summative assessment is usually linked to outcomes. In the case of the many Australian states and territories that utilise the Australian Curriculum, summative assessment is based on the achievement standards. You utilised these to create your learning objectives. Thus, by the time students complete the summative assessment, they should have been exposed to what you wanted them to know, understand and be able to do. You would have been adapting the way you approach these learning objectives, based on formative assessment data. Furthermore, you would be adapting your summative assessment to ensure it aligns with the learning objectives of the unit and the selected achievement standards.

There is a perception among many teachers, particularly those who teach secondary and senior-secondary years, that summative assessment cannot be differentiated, and that all students must receive the same assessment and conditions for fair grading (Porta, 2023). However, as established in Chapter 1, fairness does not align with equity. Differentiation in summative assessments is possible, but again, it may mean you need to rethink how you administer summative assessments. No matter the format, you can offer differentiation in summative assessment. It will mean that students could be doing things differently from one another but still be working towards the same achievement standard. Let's imagine that you were being assessed on your ability to dance, and you chose to do the tango, while another pair chose to do the quickstep. You are both demonstrating your skills in dancing, but achieving this in different ways and therefore working towards the same achievement standard. Some of the most common ways that summative assessment can be differentiated are highlighted below in Figure 38 (Tomlinson, 2014, 2022; Tomlinson & Allan, 2000).

Figure 38: Ways to differentiate summative assessment

- **Offer students choice** – allow for multiple formats such as oral, written, graphic, etc. Model these to students so they know what each format looks like, as some will be more familiar to them than others. This is where you can create summative assessments that allow students to use their learning preferences.
- **Adapt the level of complexity** – the wording of questions in tests could use simpler language for students of lower readiness or literacy levels.
- **Provide more time**, particularly in timed summative assessments, to students who require it.
- **Provide more structure** for students with lower readiness, such as further scaffolding, prompts, etc.
- **Pacing of assessment** – summative assessment does not have to be given at the end of a unit. You could break the summative assessment into sections and complete these at the end of each week. (One of my colleagues used to do this with tests, and her students' test anxiety was reduced significantly.)
- **Number of steps** – some students may prefer scaffolded steps for what to do, while others may not need a scaffold of directions.
- **Level of independence** – guide students and/or provide further instruction for students with lower readiness. Stretch students' thinking for those who have higher readiness.
- **Link to interests** – incorporate elements of students' known interests. For example, students might want to measure parts of a motorbike to determine parts that are bigger than or smaller than one another.

There is also a perception, particularly among teachers of students in senior-secondary years, that tests and exams cannot be differentiated (Porta, 2023); however, you can utilise many of the above methods to differentiate tests, exams, or other timed tasks. Personally, I provided a lot of choice in tests, moving away from students completing a standard set of questions to providing options – for example, giving students a choice of three extended response questions in a test or timed task. Similarly, in my last class, I asked students to design the end-of-semester exam questions themselves. We brainstormed questions that we thought should be asked, based on the KUDs we had covered for the unit of work. I took those questions and then moulded them into the exam. This allowed my students to have a voice in their learning, acting as a motivator and reducing test anxiety.

Using the space in Supporting Activity 8 (page 84), reflect on how you currently utilise summative assessment in your classroom. Then, create a goal for yourself that incorporates elements from Figure 38 to ensure your assessment is differentiated more. The absolute key here is that no matter what changes you make, students must be working towards the same achievement standards from the mandated curriculum. Reducing complexity does not mean that you should take away *harder* questions, or *remove* achievement standards that you think might be too complex for students. For example, in Year 3 Mathematics, the achievement standard states "they describe how stories are developed through characters and/events".

1. We need to give all students the opportunity to demonstrate this.
2. Nowhere does this say *how* students need to describe how the stories are developed. Students could do this orally or through presentation and video formats, etc.

Teachers can then make balanced judgements about the quality of learning demonstrated by students in relation to the achievement standards. Grading is possible in differentiated assessments. Students who perhaps required further support, or more scaffolding in their assessment, should not have their grade lessened. The Australian Curriculum achievement standards outline the satisfactory standard for students, and it is the teacher's role to determine if students are above, at, or below the standard based on the evidence they have collected (Australian Curriculum, Assessment and Reporting Authority, 2023c). States and territories determine their own grading systems against the achievement standards, so it is best to look at your local jurisdiction for grade interpretations.

Chapter summary and reflection

In this chapter, you have explored the second step of differentiation through understanding by design, looking at assessment evidence. I have outlined the importance of pre-assessment, formative assessment and summative assessment in differentiation, through examples, and how they play a role in ensuring that your differentiated classroom is both proactive and responsive. You have determined the importance of ensuring that assessment aligns to the learning objectives throughout the lesson and unit of work, ensuring that, in the case of summative assessment, all students have the opportunity to meet the achievement standards even when assessment is differentiated.

Take a moment now to reflect on what you have learned in this chapter using the 5R model:

1. **Report:** What are the key aspects you learned from this chapter?

   _____

   _____

   _____

2. **Respond:** How did this chapter make you feel?

   _____

   _____

   _____

3. **Relate:** What assessment practices are you currently implementing in your classroom?

   _____

   _____

   _____

4. **Reason:** How will you incorporate elements of this chapter into your existing teacher practices and philosophy?

   _____

   _____

   _____

5. **Reconstruct:** What are the main learnings from this chapter and how will you adapt in the future to ensure your classroom is proactive and responsive?

   _____

   _____

   _____

Supporting Activities

Supporting Activity 1

Pre-assessment

Supporting Activity 2

Strengths	Areas of concern

Supporting Activity 3

Students will understand that:

Students will know:

Students will be able to:

Pre-assessment:

Supporting Activity 4

Detailing a pre-assessment method.

Supporting Activity 5

Creation of pre-assessment to determine student interest.

Supporting Activity 6

Types of learner preferences.

Supporting Activity 7

Reflection on the use of formative assessment.

Supporting Activity 8

Reflection on the use of summative assessment.

Outline 1–2 goals for how you will ensure your summative assessments are differentiated.

CHAPTER 4

How *ready* are you to dance?

"It takes an athlete to dance, but an artist to be a dancer."

- SHANNA LEFLEUR

Learning objectives

By the end of this chapter:

- Teachers will understand that differentiation is made up of a set of practices that inform its philosophical approach.
- Teachers will know that the choice of strategy they implement in the classroom is dependent on the element they choose to differentiate by.
- Teachers will be able to select from a range of relevant differentiation strategies related to readiness to apply in their classrooms.

Figure 39: Backwards by design

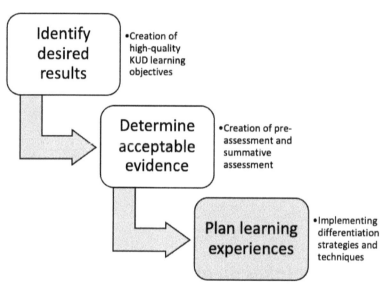

Up until now, we have really been exploring the premise of upholding quality curriculum and assessment – ensuring that our learning objectives are designed to give all students the right and the opportunity to work on age-equivalent curriculum. We have also looked at ensuring that, depending on how you are differentiating, your pre-assessments align to your learning objectives, and are determining students' readiness or interests or learning preferences at that point in time. There are *many* ways you can differentiate. Many of these are highlighted in Tomlinson's (2014) framework. We will, however, explore some of the most effective ways you can differentiate for readiness, interests and learner preferences, and I will highlight some of the ways that I have differentiated in my teaching career – both my successes and failures. For those of you who are just starting this dance of differentiation, you may find it helpful to follow my "steps" quite closely; however, I encourage you to have fun with differentiation and adapt as you see fit. This chapter focuses specifically on targeting student readiness and designing learning experiences that assist with differentiation by readiness. Chapter 5, however, focuses on designing learning experiences that target students' interests and learner preferences. Both this chapter and Chapter 5 form part of the third step of differentiation using understanding by design (Wiggins & McTighe, 2005, 2011), which is to design learning experiences.

Exploring tiered lessons

In the previous chapter you designed pre-assessments based on the learning objectives, to determine how ready students are to learn what you want to teach them. Students will have different levels of readiness, as indicated from the pre-assessments, and now you need to know what to do with such diversity. Lesson tiering is an effective method when you want to ensure that all students work towards the same learning objectives, regardless of where they are at, but you also want to provide a little more tailoring. Tiering allows you to make small changes to the lesson, to suit the different readiness levels of your students. I remind you that this does not mean that you need to make 25 different lessons to suit the 25 different learners in your class. You are going to create tiers (or groups) where you place students of similar readiness to undertake activities that are slightly different from those in other tiers.

Let's imagine you are in a dance class, and the teacher has set the learning objective that all participants will learn the waltz by the end of the class. You, along with others, bring various degrees of knowledge and skills related to doing the waltz. Your teacher gets you and your partner to attempt the waltz in the very beginning based on what you already know – this is the teachers' pre-assessment. From here, the teacher determines that some of you can dance the waltz really well, just having some minor technical challenges and issues with finesse. Some of you can waltz quite well, but make many technical mistakes throughout. While others in your class do not know how to waltz at all. This might mean that the teacher gives the students in the class who do not know how to waltz a video to watch that details the specific steps of the waltz, allowing them to practise in front of the mirror. Those who can waltz but make technical mistakes might be asked to practise their dance; however, they need to record their dancing and watch it afterwards to analyse their errors, in conjunction with reading a book that details each of the steps. Lastly, those who can waltz really well with minimal mistakes might practise, while receiving some guidance from the teacher. Hence, everyone is still working towards the same goal of dancing the waltz, but slight changes are made to address the different levels of readiness.

You might think of readiness as the student's entry point into the lesson. A crucial note here is that, at this point, you will need to consider your universal design for learning approaches too. Do not abandon this as you begin your differentiation journey. While you will be designing lessons based on readiness, and differentiating content, process and product, you must also take into account any barriers to learning that may need to be removed or minimised through universal design for learning approaches.

The first step in tiering is to consider the highest readiness tier. This is crucial as we are always aiming to *teach up* rather than teaching down. In this way, determining your higher readiness tier allows you to avoid *teaching to the middle*, as differentiation is not about adjusting up and down from the middle of the class. This practice may take some time to get used to, and you may be used to providing your *blanket* lesson, with adjustments to help students access what you are wanting most of the class to achieve. Let's always aim for the higher, to teach up, and make adjustments from there, avoiding creating learning experiences that start at the middle, with adjustments *up and down*.

You need to decide how you will differentiate at this point – whether you will differentiate by content, process or product, or a mixture of the three, while also determining what each tier will receive. I will be highlighting all three ways (content, process and product), as you progress through tiering. Always remember that students in each tier need the opportunity to meet the learning objectives. Lower tiers should not have some learning objectives removed, as this does not uphold the differentiation principles I discussed in Chapter 1. Some of the aspects you might change for your tiers are found in Figure 40. This is based on Tomlinson's (2014) equalizer, which can be used to guide your decisions. Start on the left-hand side, thinking about your higher readiness tiers first. I have only included the elements from the equalizer that I used more commonly to guide my tier construction. As you can see from each of the elements below, trying to achieve, say, a more abstract lesson for some, and a more concrete lesson for others, does not fit well within a classroom that *teaches to the middle*. This is why tiering is more effective at addressing readiness levels.

Figure 40: Elements of the equalizer by Tomlinson (2014)

Higher readiness	Lower readiness	Explanation
More abstract	More concrete	Students may be asked to focus more on meaning and relationships between concepts when dealing with the abstract. Increasing a focus to more concrete would see students focus on key information and ideas.
More complex	Simpler	Students may be asked to think about the bigger picture, with less details. They may be provided with more complex materials, resources, research, or any other means that change the complexity of the content.
More steps	Less steps	Students may be asked to complete more steps or actions, as opposed to fewer steps or actions for students who are lower readiness.
More independence	Less independence	Students in higher readiness may need less guidance from their peers or from you as the teacher. Allow the student to have more say in what and how they go about a task. Students with lower readiness may need more prescription and modelling by the teacher, and more check-ins.
Faster	Slower	Students with higher readiness explore concepts and ideas at a quicker pace, eliminating unnecessary or redundant information for the student. Students with lower readiness may need additional practice and greater depth of study.

Thinking about the changes you can make from the elements above, let's look at the example below in Figure 41. Here, you have your learning objectives and pre-assessment. From this pre-assessment, we are assuming that there are three tiers that we want to cater for in this lesson: a high readiness, middle readiness, and low readiness tier. You do not need to have three tiers;

in fact, you can have as many tiers are you feel are necessary, based on the results of your pre-assessment. However, make it manageable for you.

In the example in Figure 41, I have highlighted, in a very simplistic manner, how you might differentiate content, process and product based on the learning objectives I created from our quality curriculum. If you are not confident in tiering, I suggest you only differentiate by one area, such as process, first, before attempting to incorporate your differentiation. I have not focused on lesson timings or materials at this point, as I find that you can get lost quite quickly in determining the resources, materials and time needed for each group, losing focus on whether you are differentiating content, process or product. There has been many a time, particularly when I first started teaching, that I would create my tiers and give each tier a different task. I did not consciously think about whether I was trying to provide more concrete materials for the lower readiness groups, or whether I was giving my higher readiness groups more independence. Instead, I found that I had different tiers with different activities that worked towards the same learning goals, but no clear adjustment in difficulty or complexity. I often found myself giving more work to the higher readiness groups. By clearly outlining the changes you are making to the tiers early on, as I have done in Figure 41, your differentiation becomes more intentional, more clear, and ultimately will be more likely to target students' zone of proximal development in these tiers.

Figure 41: Lesson tiering

Achievement standard(s) and content descriptions

AS: Students explain the processes that underpin heredity and genetic diversity and describe the evidence supporting the theory of evolution by natural selection.

CD: Use the theory of evolution by natural selection to explain past and present diversity and analyse the scientific evidence supporting the theory.

Students will understand that:

- Heredity and genetic diversity are determined by a series of actions.
- Scientific theories are a way of explaining the world.
- The past has shaped the diversity in the world.

Students will know:

- How the theory of natural selection can explain evolution
- How natural selection contributes to diversity in populations.

Students will be able to:

- Use scientific theories
- Explain the impact of the past and present on diversity
- Analyse scientific evidence.

Pre-assessment (for readiness)

1. Provide an example that illustrates how natural selection acts to shape genetic diversity within a population.
2. How did the theory of natural selection come about and how does it connect with evolution?

Content differentiation

- **Tier 1 (low readiness):** Offer use of simplified readings, pulling out key terminology and definitions. Have students use a Punnett square to showcase their understanding of basic genetic principles.

- **Tier 2 (middle readiness):** Offer simplified explanations using visuals, diagrams and simplified readings to engage understanding of basic genetic principles. Offer guided practice to help students navigate scientific evidence supporting evolution.

- **Tier 3 (high readiness):** Offer a more advanced reading or resource that delves deeper into heredity and genetic diversity, and provide these students with scientific evidence supporting evolution to debate upon.

Process differentiation

- **Tier 1 (low readiness):** Offer students a scaffold and YouTube videos regarding heredity and natural selection. The scaffold guides students to outline elements of heredity and natural selection. Students in this tier use the notes from their scaffold to discuss the theory of natural selection, with teacher guidance.

- **Tier 2 (middle readiness):** Offer students in this tier some visual supports. Students are given a series of images of animals that have changed over time, such as the Galapagos finches. Students in this tier use these images to describe the changes to the finches, using the internet to support their ideas.

- **Tier 3 (high readiness):** Offer students in this tier a critical thinking task that asks them to critically analyse and synthesise scientific evidence supporting evolution by natural selection. Students in this tier are not offered potential sources of evidence; however, you may provide some example case studies.

Product differentiation

- **Tier 1 (low readiness):** Offer students the opportunity to create a written summary or concept maps, highlighting the basic concepts of heredity and natural selection. A comprehensive list of scientific sources is provided to these students to guide the construction of their concept map or summary. Students are guided more frequently by the teacher.
- **Tier 2 (middle readiness):** Offer students the opportunity to create a presentation on an animal that has evolved over time. Students in this tier are provided with an optional scaffolded PowerPoint presentation, some example animals, and a list of some sources of evidence to support their presentation. This may be done in small groups or pairs.
- **Tier 3 (high readiness):** Offer students in this tier the opportunity to create a video documentary showcasing their understanding of evolution and natural selection. Students complete this in pairs, taking on the role of David Attenborough, highlighting an example of an animal and how it has evolved over time. Students need to find scientific evidence in this tier.

Using the space in Supporting Activity 1 (page 104), and looking back at the tiered science lesson in Figure 41, what do you notice about each of the tiers I designed? How are they different? For example, do the tiers show a clear change in independence, with more independence offered to the higher tier? You may want to use the following from the New South Wales Government (2022) outlining ways you can tier instruction and activities.

Figure 42: NSW Government tiering considerations

Activities and assignments can be adjusted by:

- Level of complexity
- Amount of structure
- Materials provided
- Time allowed
- Pacing of the assignment
- Number of steps required for completion
- Form of expression – for example, letter, essay, report, research paper, short story, speech
- Level of independence required.

As you can see from the tiered lesson in Figure 41, this is a very simplistic view of differentiation of content, process and product. You will, as you naturally see fit, provide opportunities for whole-class or explicit instruction, and other pedagogies where necessary, opportunities for class closure and openings that perhaps introduce the lesson focus or focus on key points covered in the lesson. With the content differentiation, my aim here was to increase the complexity of the text or readings, for certain tiers. I used to do this a lot, particularly when I taught Year 10 English. I was often frustrated that the class had to read the same text, knowing that students' readiness and literacy levels were of varying degrees. So, when it came time to read Macbeth the following year, I found three different text types:

1. The original play written in Shakespearean language
2. The Shakespearean play with English translations included
3. A simpler version written in plain English and including pictures.

What ensued was outstanding. The students were grouped according to readiness, and these groups lasted the term. We could keep pace as a class, as I would often assign a particular scene each lesson. As each tier had covered the same content, just in varying degrees of complexity, I could then create mixed-readiness groups, allowing students to discuss with other students who had a different perspective from them. This was one of my proudest tiering moments, because I could see that students engaged with the text they had received but still felt part of the class, no matter which text they had. Did I have to abandon the idea that I had always used the same text for all students, having them read aloud in class as one large group? Yes! And it was uncomfortable because this method was so engrained in my teaching; however, that slight change in text made my classroom even more accessible. Similarly, I offered the audiobook to students in any tier, for those who preferred to listen, allowing me to increase the accessibility even more, utilising principles of universal design for learning.

You can see with the differentiation of process in Figure 41 that I have provided a few different ways for students to meet the same end goal. For my lower readiness tier, who demonstrated some gaps in knowledge and understanding of heredity and natural selection, I gave them a YouTube video to watch to help supplement the content. Similarly, I am guiding my middle readiness tier with a series of images of well-known animals, like the Galapagos Island finches, which highlight natural selection. However, my higher readiness tier likely does not need the video or the images, given that they have shown a good understanding in the pre-test. Again, having these tiers does not mean you need to abandon your whole-class instruction – in fact, you may only have students in their tiers for part of the lesson, before continuing on as a whole class on another task or activity.

Lastly, product differentiation in the science lesson meant that I could adjust the complexity of the output for students. For example, the higher readiness tier was tasked with creating a documentary, taking on the role of someone like David Attenborough, showcasing an example of natural selection. If this was going to be over multiple lessons, I might increase the requirements, such as including more video editing, etc. If the output was expected in one lesson, I might have students use Microsoft Flip or Canva to create a simplified version of a documentary. Similarly, for my lower readiness tiers, the output has also been reduced in complexity, from a presentation to a written summary.

Using the space provided in Supporting Activity 2 (page 104), you can now start to create your own tiered lesson plan, consisting of at least three tiers for high, medium and low readiness. You have already made learning objectives and pre-assessments to match; now you can outline the three tiers. Determine whether you will use content, process or product (or a mixture of the three) in your lesson. As you begin to make your way through designing a tiered lesson plan, ask yourself these questions to ensure your lesson is tiered effectively (Figure 43).

Figure 43: Questions to ask yourself when tiering

1. What are the readiness levels in my classroom?
2. Are the learning objectives clear, comprehensive and aligned to the mandated curriculum?
3. Are the learning objectives allowing students to demonstrate what they know, understand and can do?
4. Have I pre-assessed my students against the learning objectives (for readiness) and what determines who goes into each tier?
5. Have I started with the highest tier, teaching up?
6. What activities, resources and materials can I use that are suitable for each tier?
7. How will I monitor student progress?
8. How can I support each readiness tier?
9. How will I measure the effectiveness of each tier?

Flexible grouping

While you have been exploring tiering, flexible grouping is largely responsible for allowing you to construct those tiers in the first place. Flexible grouping is a key premise in differentiation, and utilising flexible groups allows you to group students by readiness, interests or learning preferences, or a mixture of them. Many of you will be more confident in utilising flexible grouping than others and, much like differentiation, flexible grouping takes time to master. This is so for both the teacher and the students. Some students may not be used to being grouped by the teacher, let alone grouped in a variety of ways, so grouping should start small. Simply grouping students based on convenience, or assigning different groups different work, is not differentiation.

For effective differentiation to occur, flexible grouping needs to be intentional! I can genuinely say that flexible grouping was, and still is, my most-used differentiation practice in all of my classrooms. It really allowed me to divide my time across the whole classroom, having students work together in groups, consult and support each other, all while I could roam around to each group, offering further guidance to those who were struggling or in the lower readiness groups. Doubet (2022) asks you to consider the following when utilising flexible grouping (Figure 44).

Figure 44: Aspects to consider when using flexible grouping

1. **The purpose of the flexible grouping**
   Ask yourself, "What educational purpose will grouping serve right now?"

2. **Duration**
   Ask yourself, "How long will it take for this group to achieve its purpose?"

3. **Student characteristics**
   Ask yourself, "What student characteristics matter for this task or learning experience? Readiness/interests? Learner preferences?"

4. **Composition**
   Ask yourself, "Should the groups be constructed with the characteristics identified earlier in mind and be homogenous or heterogenous?"

5. **Configuration and size**
   Ask yourself, "What size makes the most sense, given the learning activity's goals and our particular circumstances?"

6. **Formation**
   Ask yourself, "Who will determine the groups? The teacher? Students?"

SOURCE: DOUBET (2022).

By now, you have heard me say this multiple times, but simply putting students in groups is not flexible grouping. Flexible grouping must have a purpose (Doubet, 2022). For example, the way you group students who are working on a project together, compared to students examining a data set, could be different, as these two activities serve a different purpose from one another. Knowing the purpose will assist you in determining the other factors outlined in Figure 44. Consider students working on a large project together: the duration of the project is likely going to be longer than students who are examining a data set. It may be that the students working on the project are grouped in this way for over a week, while those examining the data set could be in a group for 20 minutes of the lesson. The more complex the task or activity, the longer the duration of the group. Similarly, and this goes without saying, you need to know how you intend to differentiate (content, process, product) and according to what (readiness, interests, learner preferences) and whether you intend to group in homogenous or heterogenous compositions. For example, while you have been learning about tiering, which is essentially grouping students with similar readiness levels, you may want to group students with varying levels of readiness, whereby students can learn from one another, offering a range of perspectives. This is similar to having students work together with different interests, which could increase their engagement and motivation (Doubet, 2022). Lastly, you need to think about the size of your groups. For students who are not accustomed to working in groups, it is best to start small. Even for you as teacher, if you are not confident with group work, consider starting small with partners and trios. Again, the purpose of your groups will help to determine the size. For example, robust discussions could be served best with larger groups, while grouping with the purpose of students getting to know one another could be better served in pairs.

When I was conducting research for my PhD, I found that teachers with high self-efficacy in differentiation implementation tended to involve students more in their differentiation decisions (Porta, 2023), with students driving the lesson. Deciding whether you or your students will determine the grouping is another decision you need to make. Obviously, as teacher, you are best positioned to gather student data and identify what each student needs to grow; hence, you will likely form the groups. However, students can form their own groups, and you may want to add in some parameters when they do so, to ensure no student is left out.

Read the following case study in Figure 45 of a teacher who utilised flexible grouping in her Year 6 Science lesson. As you read through the case study, consider the aspects outlined by Doubet (2022) in Figure 44. Has the teacher considered these elements when undertaking flexible grouping? How has the teacher differentiated? Outline your thoughts in Supporting Activity 3 (page 104).

Figure 45: Flexible grouping case study – Mrs Thompson

In preparing for the Science lesson on ecosystems, Mrs Thompson considered several factors when employing flexible grouping. Understanding the importance of group dynamics, she deliberately kept the group sizes small, ensuring meaningful interaction and individual participation. The formation of these groups was purpose-driven, based on data from ongoing assessments, previous observations and student preferences. Mrs Thompson designed the flexible groups with a clear purpose: to address varying readiness levels effectively.

In the high readiness group, she curated advanced research tasks focusing on intricate ecosystem interactions. Students here engaged in in-depth investigations using scientific journals, online resources and complex readings. Their task was to explore symbiotic relationships within ecosystems and present their findings through a detailed report or presentation.

The middle readiness group concentrated on identifying and understanding basic ecosystem components. Mrs Thompson provided simplified readings, diagrams and structured activities to scaffold their learning. Students worked collaboratively to identify and classify primary elements of ecosystems, utilising visual aids and simplified texts to reinforce their understanding.

For the low readiness group, Mrs Thompson employed hands-on activities, visual aids and direct guidance. These students participated in interactive tasks, such as sorting and categorising visual representations of ecosystem components. Guided by Mrs Thompson, they focused on recognising basic elements and building foundational knowledge through interactive learning experiences.

Each group was working towards the same learning objectives. The duration of the flexible grouping was structured to allow for an optimal balance between engagement and focus. Mrs Thompson allocated adequate time for each group to explore the tasks, ensuring ample opportunity for meaningful learning experiences while maintaining a sense of pace within the lesson. This approach allowed her to cater to diverse learning needs, foster collaboration and empower each student to progress at their own pace.

Throughout the lesson, Mrs Thompson rotated among the groups, providing targeted support, clarification and extension activities as needed. By tailoring the tasks and support mechanisms to suit the readiness levels, she ensured that each student received a meaningful and appropriately challenging learning experience.

During my time as a teacher, I was lucky enough to be nationally recognised as a Highly Accomplished Teacher by undergoing certification through AITSL. Much of my evidence was linked towards assisting teachers to be more inclusive and to become more confident in differentiation. As a result of certification, AITSL filmed one of my lessons, which I provided commentary on, highlighting differentiation in my Year 11 and 12 compositive Business Innovation class. You can view the full lesson here: https://www.aitsl.edu.au/teach/improve-practice/in-the-classroom/differentiation

In this lesson, I highlight the use of flexible grouping, differentiating the process for the groups, which consisted of students of similar readiness levels. I wanted students to develop deeper knowledge of value proposition, looking specifically at what customers need and want. I knew many of my students had completed Business Innovation before, while others were new to the course, hence the varying levels of readiness. I encourage you to watch this lesson, particularly with my commentary, as you can delve deeply into the flexible grouping decisions I made for that lesson.

Use of curriculum compacting

When I first learned about curriculum compacting, I must admit, I was overwhelmed. I thought, "I haven't even mastered how to tier yet, let alone compact the curriculum." The thing about curriculum compacting is that it does make sense. Why waste valuable teaching time on teaching something that some students may already know, understand or be able to do? Why not use that time to extend and challenge students even further. Ideally, you will know from the results of your pre-assessment which students already know, understand and can do, in relation to your learning objectives. Curriculum compacting is particularly useful for students who are highly able, or consistently demonstrate high readiness, with the aim of extending and challenging them. The steps for curriculum compacting, adapted from Renzulli and Reis (1992) and Reis and Renzulli (2005), are outlined in Figure 46. Within these steps, create your learning objectives and pre-assessment to determine who your higher readiness students are. You may choose to provide tiered learning activities for these students, or not; however, the aim here is not to provide *busy work* or more work, per se. You want to spark interest and creativity, extending students' knowledge and skills in relation to the learning objectives. You might consider more self-directed learning opportunities, or more collaborative learning with similar readiness students.

Figure 46: Steps to curriculum compacting

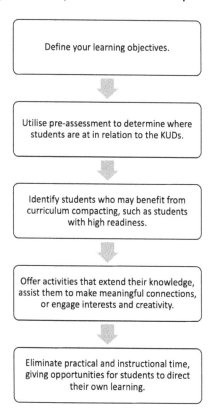

One of the ways that you may want to provide extra challenge to your students who have been identified as possibly benefiting from curriculum compacting may be through the Australian Curriculum General Capabilities. There are seven general capabilities that form part of the Australian Curriculum. The general capabilities "equip young Australians with the knowledge, skills, behaviours and dispositions to live and work successfully" (Australian Curriculum Assessment and Reporting Authority, 2023b, para. 1).

The seven capabilities are:

1. Critical and creative thinking
2. Digital literacy
3. Ethical understanding
4. Intercultural understanding
5. Literacy
6. Numeracy
7. Personal and social capability.

I believe that the Version 9 Australian Curriculum capabilities can be of significant use here in extending students who may require further challenge. In fact, the Australian Curriculum, Assessment and Reporting Authority outlines that the teaching of learning area content will be strengthened by the application of relevant general capabilities (Australian Curriculum, Assessment and Reporting Authority, 2023b). Let's take this example of a content description for Year 4 English:

> **AC9E4LY05** – use comprehension strategies such as visualising, predicting, connecting, summarising, monitoring and questioning to build literal and inferred meaning, to expand topic knowledge and ideas, and evaluate texts

As part of the literacy capability, teachers will need to use the following literacy capability (Level 6 – listening) through the teaching of this content description, as outlined in Figure 47. Hence, when asking students to build literacy and inferred meaning within text, Level 6 of the capability says that students should be able to infer layered meaning from text and identify the purpose of spoken text and the intended audience of the spoken text. Hence, students are developing their listening skills by engaging in the above content. However, you may have determined that many of your higher readiness students can do this already, when analysing your pre-assessment data. Therefore, you may choose to provide challenge by still teaching the selected content description, achievement standard and learning objectives derived from these, but increasing the complexity through the capabilities.

Figure 47: Level 6 – listening

Level 6
- responds to moderately complex texts (see Text complexity)
- responds to texts with unfamiliar content
- identifies main ideas of a spoken text using supporting details

- identifies purpose and intended audience of a spoken text
- infers layered meaning from texts (e.g. musical overlay that creates mood)
- asks relevant questions to extend understanding
- describes language and audio features of the text

For example, let's look at the difference between Level 6 – listening, as part of the literacy capability, and the next level, Level 7 – listening, as shown in Figure 48. This time, there is an increase in challenge and complexity. Instead of asking your higher readiness students to identify the purpose and intended audience of a spoken text (Level 6), you might design your activity or higher readiness tier to ask these students to analyse how the spoken language is used. Using the capabilities takes significant skill and understanding of how the capabilities work within the Australian Curriculum, and what they mean. Using the capabilities in a siloed approach should be avoided – that is to say, you should not just focus on teaching capabilities on their own, without the content from the relevant subject. The capabilities are "best developed within, specific learning areas; others support learning in any learning area. General capabilities are identified in content descriptions where they are developed or applied through learning area content" (Australian Curriculum, Assessment and Reporting Authority, 2023b, para. 3); hence do not take a siloed approach.

Figure 48: Level 7 – listening

Level 7
- responds to complex texts (see Text complexity)
- identifies and analyses how spoken laqnguage is used for different effects
- explains the use of intonation, pausing, rhythm and phrasing to give emphasis and weight to ideas
- selects appropriate listening strategies for planned and unplanned situations (e.g. records and organises information from a text in a table or with detailed notes)
- explains how vocabulary is used for impact on the target audience

Curriculum compacting will not apply to all students, nor will it be required in every lesson. This is really for students who have demonstrated that they have mastered the learning objectives to a very high level, meaning that they have the skills to delve deeper into more advanced or challenging topics, engage in enrichment activities, pursue independent projects, or receive specialised instruction tailored to their interests. Let's take a look at the case study of Ms Rodriguez, outlined in Figure 49, who has utilised curriculum compacting in her Science class.

Figure 49: Case study of curriculum compacting

Scenario: Science class – exploring genetics

Ms Rodriguez teaches a diverse group of eighth-grade students who are currently studying genetics. The unit includes topics such as heredity, genetic traits, Punnett squares, and the basics of DNA.

Step 1: Pre-assessment:

Ms Rodriguez starts the genetics unit with a pre-assessment to gauge what students know, understand and can do. She designs a quiz that covers fundamental genetics concepts, including Punnett squares, dominant and recessive traits, and basic genetic inheritance.

Step 2: Identifying higher readiness students:

Upon reviewing the pre-assessment results, Ms Rodriguez identifies several students who exhibit a strong understanding of the introductory genetics concepts. These students demonstrate proficiency in predicting genetic outcomes using Punnett squares and understanding Mendelian inheritance patterns.

Step 3: Tailoring curriculum for advanced learners:

For the advanced learners, Ms Rodriguez implements curriculum compacting by providing enriched and extended learning opportunities:

- She offers advanced assignments that delve deeper into genetics concepts, such as exploring complex inheritance patterns or researching contemporary genetic advancements.
- The students are given the option to pursue independent research projects on topics such as genetic engineering, gene-editing technologies like CRISPR, or the ethical implications of genetic discoveries.
- Ms Rodriguez designs lab experiments that challenge advanced students to apply their understanding of genetics in more complex scenarios, such as conducting hands-on gene expression studies.

Step 4: Ongoing support and enrichment:

Ms Rodriguez ensures ongoing support for advanced learners by providing resources; however, she reduces the instructional time for these students, allowing them to have some independence in what they learn.

Now, it is your turn! Using the space in Supporting Activity 4 (page 104) and learning objectives of your choosing, I want you to imagine that you have pre-assessed your class, and some students have demonstrated that they are eligible for curriculum compacting. Outline how you will compact the curriculum and how you will extend these students, while still working towards the same learning objectives. You may want to consult the ACARA website (https://www.acara.edu.au/curriculum), to utilise the general capabilities. Think about activities, resources, etc.

Chapter summary and reflection

In this chapter, you have explored differentiation according to readiness, specifically looking at tiered lessons and how to go about creating meaningful tiers that address readiness. You have developed a deeper understanding of flexible grouping and the purposeful nature behind flexible grouping in the differentiated classroom. Furthermore, you have learned about curriculum compacting, and how the general capabilities can be applied to extend and challenge students who are of higher readiness, while still teaching the relevant curriculum content. Using the template below, reflect on the key learnings from this chapter.

What surprised me?

_____

_____

What was one key takeaway from this chapter?

_____

_____

Where will I go from here?

_____

_____

What do I need to change or adapt?

_____

_____

Supporting Activity 1

Analysis of differentiation within the science lesson

Supporting Activity 2

Creation of a tiered lesson plan (use separate page/s for this)

Supporting Activity 3

Reflection on flexible grouping – Mrs Thompson

Supporting Activity 4

Curriculum compacting

CHAPTER 5

Can I *interest* you in a *preferred* dance?

"Any kind of dancing is better than no dancing at all."

– LYNDA BARR

Learning objectives

By the end of this chapter:

- Teachers will understand that differentiation is made up of a set of practices and principles that inform its philosophical approach.
- Teachers will know that the choice of strategy they implement in the classroom is dependent on the element they choose to differentiate by.
- Teachers will be able to select from a range of relevant differentiation strategies related to students' interests and learning preferences to apply in their classrooms.

Figure 50: Backwards by design

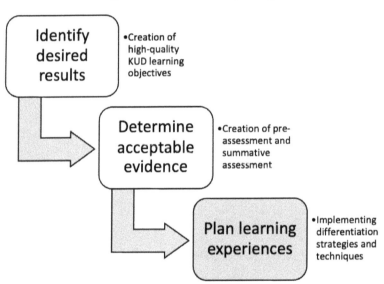

In the previous chapter, we explored differentiation through readiness, creating learning experiences through the understanding by design approach (Wiggins & McTighe, 2005, 2011) to cater to varying levels of student readiness. In this chapter, we continue with the creation of differentiated learning experiences; however, our attention will shift from readiness to differentiation according to students' interests and learner preferences. I will highlight common differentiation techniques for interests and learner preferences, such as a learning menu and RAFTs; however, I want to make it very clear that utilisation of these techniques is not exclusive to differentiation. You can create differentiated assessment tasks or activities according to interests or learner preferences beyond the learning menu and RAFT. In fact, in Chapter 1, I outlined Tomlinson's (2014) framework in which she suggests a range of ways you can implement differentiation, but again, you are not limited to these. It might sound obvious, but when you utilise students' interests in the classroom, you allow students to be more engaged (Tomlinson & Borland, 2022) and you allow other students to learn about interests beyond their own. Similarly, students have preferences in the way they want to approach a particular assignment or task or demonstrate their learning, and these preferences change – your aim is to provide ways that students can demonstrate what they know in a way that helps them make sense of the content they have been learning.

Using students' interests does not mean that you need to make every activity or task match what they like or are interested in. When I first started trying to embed student interests, I felt a great deal of pressure trying to incorporate each student's interests into tasks. I felt like I was spending a considerable amount of time trying to get it right and not disappoint my students. There are also only so many times you can embed Pokémon into a task! I found that I focused too much on targeting student interests, without ensuring that they were exposed to other students' interests too. A significant benefit with the Version 9 Australian Curriculum is that many of the content descriptions are broad enough that you can embed interests. For example, in Year 6 Humanities and Social Sciences (HASS), one of the content descriptions is: "AC9HS6S02 – locate, collect and organise information and data from primary and secondary sources in a range of formats". This is a perfect example of where you have the flexibility to find out students' historical interests, utilising primary and secondary sources in those interest areas, for students to organise. This example is just one of many.

Much like student interests, I went a little mad trying to embed a range of learner preferences into my activities and tasks. The challenge, however, was not the embedding of learner preferences but the pushback I received from other teachers. I taught Year 10 English for a number of years, alongside six other teachers. Nearly all of our summative assessment tasks were essays – we did not provide students with any opportunity for oral presentation, videos, TikTok-style assessments, etc. Even worse, when I wanted to offer these multiple ways for students to demonstrate, I was met with the argument: "It is not fair if others do presentations (for example), compared to essays. How will we grade them fairly?" It was frustrating. This view was strengthened as I began teaching Year 11 and 12 subjects, where many teachers felt constrained by the senior-secondary curriculum, stating that in many cases, they had to complete examinations or timed tasks (Porta, 2023). I am here to tell you that you have flexibility and that you can differentiate such tasks by providing options for learner preferences. It may mean educating your fellow colleagues on the difference between fairness and equity, as outlined in Chapter 1. Again, this takes a shift in mindset and a willingness to change the way of teaching that you are perhaps used to. Whenever I teach my undergraduate students, I ask them: "If I want to know if my students know the difference between a cat and a dog, and some of them do this verbally, while others write out the differences, then both sets of students have shown me they know the difference between cats and dogs, just in different ways". Allow yourself to move away from providing a one-size-fits-all approach to your classroom. This takes courage!

Let's take this achievement standard from the Version 9 Australian Curriculum for Year 10 Mathematics: "They solve measurement problems involving surface area and volume of composite objects."

Where does it say that students must demonstrate this in test form? It doesn't. I could have students use graphic organisers, worksheets, recordings etc. in demonstrating this achievement standard. Hence, students' learning preferences can be used here. The challenge for you as the teacher is to decide when to use learner preferences and when not to use learner preferences, balancing preferred and non-preferred modalities.

Learning menus

A learning menu is a versatile tool used in differentiation, offering students a variety of learning options to explore specific topics or concepts. Much like a restaurant menu, learning menus present a range of activities or tasks from which students can choose, based on their learning preferences, interests or readiness. These menus often feature a mix of activities designed to accommodate diverse learning modalities and interests. A learning menu typically includes different categories or types of tasks, such as appetisers (introductory tasks), main courses (core learning activities) and desserts (enrichment or extension tasks). Each task is aligned with specific learning objectives, enabling students to engage with the content in ways that resonate with them personally.

The beauty of a learning menu lies in its flexibility and ability to encourage student autonomy. It allows students to select activities that match their interests or cater to their preferred learning preferences, empowering them to take ownership of their learning journey. Additionally, these menus promote self-regulation and independence as students navigate through the various tasks, fostering a sense of responsibility for their education. Learning menus take considerable planning time, and there is a reason for this. You need to ensure alignment between the tasks offered in the menu and the learning objectives derived from the curriculum. Where people fall down, is that they may offer a range of menu items that cater to interests, learner preferences or readiness, but do not put in any parameters, meaning that some students may meet all learning objectives, while others may only meet a few, depending on the tasks they select. Careful planning is needed here!

Now I will be the first to admit that while the learning menu in Figure 51 looks like it has been differentiated well, and I perhaps thought I had differentiated, I likely had not. However, I am showing you, as had I taken a few steps beforehand, then it would have been differentiated well, according to learner preferences. This learning menu was designed for my Year 11 Psychology class, and was designed to run for about four weeks. I designed my main courses to be compulsory – these were recorded videos of content on each of the areas of human psychological development, and embedded in these videos were quizzes and multiple-choice questions. I could see the results of these quizzes, further influencing the activities I guided my students to do. The side dishes were where I embedded student choice. While there were a variety of preferences embedded within the side dishes, I did not pre-assess for these at the time. Therefore, they were not really differentiated by learner preferences, and therefore it was not really differentiation. Had I done so, I could have been more targeted in my approach and more effective in my differentiation.

The side dishes were a great opportunity for students to consolidate what they had learned in the main tasks. When I was meeting students, I could use the results of the video quizzes, discussions with the students, and other activities to guide students to complete certain activities. For example, creating a diagram of Erikson's theory was more challenging than the match-up task. One aspect that needed significant improvement with this learning menu was alignment to the learning objectives. While I had clear KUD goals, I quickly realised that some of the choices students made in the learning menu exempted them from some learning objectives. This was poor differentiation on my part. All students need to have the opportunity to meet the learning objectives, no matter the choices made in the learning menu.

Figure 51: Example learning menu for Year 11 Psychology

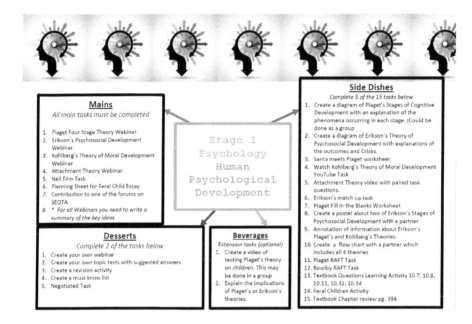

I provided dessert options as a means to increase student collaboration with one another, so students had to complete two of the choices and another student had to undertake them. For example, student 1 would write a revision activity, and student 2 would undertake this. Lastly, the beverages were extension activities for students who required extension. Looking back at these, I could have been more intentional about what challenge I wanted to provide, as they became more busy work than true extension and challenge.

When I first started learning menus, I was very much about *hard copy*. I made little folders for each of my students, with print-outs of each of the activities that students could select to engage in. As the years progressed, I took more of a digital approach, creating a Microsoft OneNote, where all of the activities, tasks, instructions and resources were located. While this planning took a considerable amount of time up front, there was a payoff to this during the four weeks my students were working on these. I had a class of 25 at the time, with two 1.5-hour lessons and a 45-minute lesson per week. This meant that I had around about 9 minutes to spend with each student individually. This was incredibly valuable time. I could give them feedback on their progress and the activities they had completed, further guiding them to activities that may have been better suited to their readiness levels. If I were to do this differently, I would have even had my check-ins as groups rather than individuals. Here, students could learn from one another and give feedback to each other, further enhancing collaboration and self-regulation.

Using the space in Supporting Activity 1 (page 122), start by planning out a potential learning menu for a selected class. Determine your learning objectives from your mandated curriculum, and decide whether you will differentiate by readiness, interest, learner preferences or a combination of the three. Think about what activities you will provide for each of the sections of the menu.

RAFTs

Another common strategy for differentiation outlined by Tomlinson (2014) are RAFTs (Role, Audience, Format, Topic). RAFTs are incredibly valuable in differentiation; in fact, they allow teachers to differentiate according to interests and learner preferences, much like the learning menu. You can add students' interests into the topic, while adding their learner preferences into the RAFT format. Take the example RAFT in Figure 52. A range of learner preferences has been embedded into this RAFT within the format – for this to be differentiated, the teacher would have needed to have assessed students' preferences beforehand, rather than making assumptions about what the teacher thinks those preferences would be. Similarly, a range of interests could have been targeted here. Mutualism, commensalism and parasitism are examples of symbiotic relationships, relationships in which many animals and plants engage. The teacher could have assessed students' interests in animals and plants, incorporating these into the audience and topic of the RAFT.

Figure 52: Example RAFT

Role	Audience	Format	Topic
Clownfish	Sea anemone	Persuasive letter	We need each other (mutualism)
Whales	Barnacles	Diary entries	It is time for you to leave (commensalism)
Human	Tapeworm	Home evacuation letter	Leave me alone (parasitism)

Where people often fall short is that they provide options that are not aligned with the learning objectives for the lesson or unit. This means that, depending on what students choose, they may not all be able to show what they know, understand and can do in relation to the learning objectives. This was similar with the learning menu discussed earlier. Again, no matter the choice of RAFT a student makes, they should have the opportunity to meet all learning objectives.

Using the space in Supporting Activity 2 (page 123), start by planning out your learning objectives for a potential RAFT. This RAFT could go for one lesson, or it might be something students work on for an extended period of time. Use the space to detail a pre-assessment that will determine students' interests and learner preferences, which you can then use to create your RAFT. Administer the pre-assessment and then revisit this supporting activity to design the RAFT using student data. While I have utilised RAFTs many times, I have adapted them to suit my own needs, extending them to a few more elements. Using the CREATE acronym, I have adapted this from a RAFT comprising the following elements:

Figure 53: CREATE framework for interests and learner preferences

CREATE

- **C – Choice of context:** students choose the context or setting in which they want to explore the content. For example, they might choose a historical period, futuristic world, particular industry or different planet.
- **R – Roles and relationships:** students can select or create characters, professions or personas that resonate with their interests. They can define the roles, perspectives, challenges or goals related to the topic.
- **E – Expression and end products:** students are offered various modes of expression or end products to showcase their learning. This could include digital storytelling, podcasts, TikTok-style creations, videos, infographics, debates or artistic representations. This allows for differentiation of product.
- **A – Audience and authenticity:** instead of specifying a particular audience, students are encouraged to consider the authenticity and relevance of their work. They might present their projects to a chosen audience, whether it be peers, younger students, professionals or even an online community interested in the topic.
- **T– Technology integration:** students need to utilise a form of technology in the task. Some students might prefer different digital platforms to others, allowing them to utilise their learning preferences.

- **E – Exploration of interests:** students explore personal interests, such as hobbies, passions or other areas of curiosity, in their project, to make it more meaningful and engaging for them.

Below are two examples of the create framework used for History and Science (Figure 54). This is not something that I would typically do in one lesson, but over an extended period of time. While this framework allows you to address interests and learner preferences, you could pre-assess for readiness, and group students according to their readiness levels; however, this detracts from their interests and learner preferences. This is your decision to make.

Figure 54: Example of the CREATE framework for differentiation

History
- **Choice of context:** students choose a historical event (World War II, the Renaissance, the Industrial Revolution) as the context for their project.
- **Roles and relationships:** they adopt roles like soldiers, artists, inventors or political figures and explore the event from those perspectives.
- **Expression and end products:** students create a series of diary entries from the viewpoint of their chosen roles, compile a documentary-style video, or design a virtual museum exhibition.
- **Audience and authenticity:** they present their projects to classmates in a historical "symposium" or publish their work online for a wider audience interested in the historical period.
- **Technology integration:** they use digital platforms for research and presentation, but they could also create physical artifacts or paintings to complement their projects.
- **Exploration of interests:** students incorporate personal interests like art, music or literature from the specific historical era into their projects.

Science
- **Choice of context:** select a scientific phenomenon such as photosynthesis, the water cycle or chemical reactions as the core topic.
- **Roles and relationships:** assume roles of different elements or molecules involved and explain interactions from their perspective.
- **Expression and end products:** create a stop-motion animation, a digital interactive simulation, a comic strip series explaining the scientific process, or a live experiment demonstration.

- **Audience and authenticity:** share their projects to a panel of science teachers.
- **Technology integration:** use virtual labs for experiments or models for representation, but also have the option to create physical models or conduct hands-on experiments.
- **Exploration of interests:** integrate personal hobbies or interests (like drawing, music or gaming) into explaining scientific concepts.

Differentiated assessment tasks

As I briefly outlined at the beginning of the chapter, many of the teachers in my research felt a tension between *getting through content* and providing differentiated assessment tasks, feeling restricted, and having a sense that, by not providing all students with the same assessment task, this was somehow unfair to other students. As we established in Chapter 1, fairness is not equity. Depending on the achievement standard you are using, you can offer students a variety of choices in the way they present their assessment task. Students do not all need to do the same, and the achievement standards for the Version 9 Australian Curriculum are written in a way that gives you such flexibility. Let's take the following achievement standard for Year 10 English: "By the end of Year 10, students interact with others, and listen to and create spoken and multimodal texts including literary texts. With a range of purposes and for audiences, they discuss ideas and responses to representations, making connections and providing substantiation." Nowhere here does it say that students need to demonstrate this achievement standard in a certain format; hence, this gives you the freedom to target learner preferences. I want to challenge you to think about the terminology you use in your rubrics. For example, if your rubric includes a reference to students completing a *written* task, then of course, if students do not do a written task, they are disadvantaged. Keep your terminology broad – use words such as *selected output* or *chosen format*, as I have done in a section of a rubric I created in Figure 55.

You have to shift your mindset when differentiating assessment. It is OK to have students working on different activities with different formats, with some students provided with more or less scaffolding, fewer steps, or greater complexity of resources. It may mean you need to let go of what you have seen others do in their classrooms, or what you yourself have been doing for assessment, and it may mean that you need to educate your fellow colleagues on what differentiated assessment means. Again, you need to be really clear about what the outcomes are that all students are expected to achieve and work backwards from there. At the end of the day, the point of summative assessment is for students to demonstrate what they know, understand and can do, with reference to the relevant achievement standards. Tomlinson (2005) herself argued that there is a perception that there is incompatibility between differentiation and summative assessment with grading, citing poor understanding of the principles of differentiation. She said it perfectly when she acknowledged "from the perspective of quality grading, there is nothing unfair about providing multiple pathways and support systems for learning. What matters is ensuring clarity and stability in criteria we will use to teach, construct assessments and measure success" (p. 266). You might be wondering, however, why I have discussed differentiated assessment in a chapter on interests and learner preferences. I chose to do this because I want to stress the importance of ensuring that learner preferences and interests are embedded into assessment tasks – that students do not all have to use the same format of test or oral presentation to meet the Australian Curriculum achievement standards. Certainly, you can differentiate assessment tasks according to readiness too. You have designed tiered lesson plans, and there is nothing to say that you cannot tier assessment tasks as well, as long as you ensure that all students have the opportunity to meet the selected achievement standards.

Figure 55: Example of section of a rubric

Criteria	A (Excellent)	B (Good)	C (Satisfactory)	D (Basic)	E (Limited)
Output	Produces sophisticated and innovative output, displaying a deep understanding of purpose, audience, and content.	Creates well-developed output showing a clear understanding of purpose and audience.	Creates adequate output, but with occasional inconsistencies in purpose or audience awareness.	Creates basic output with limited consideration for purpose and audience.	Produces very basic output, demonstrating minimal understanding of purpose and audience.

There is also a bigger battle here with differentiated assessments – in many instances, you will be teaching the same subject as others, and you may feel pressure from faculty colleagues to follow the same assessment task as other classes. If you feel this pressure, take the time to work with your colleagues to help them understand fairness and equity, and explain that providing differentiated assessment tasks actually means you can provide a more meaningful learning experience and address diversity in your classrooms more effectively. You will receive pushback – in nearly all of my roles, when I have wanted to offer a variety of formats to my students, I have received such pushback, particularly from teachers who were comfortable with administering assessment tasks they had repeated over and over again. Even when multiple formats were offered, there was an unconscious bias towards making students select a preferred format of the teacher. I will never forget arguing with a faculty leader for English, advocating that we needed to allow students multiple formats to demonstrate their knowledge, with which they disagreed. As a compromise, they added "to be completed as an 800-word essay or multimodal". You might be thinking, "Well that's progress, isn't it?" Well, it might have been, except for the fact that students were provided with exemplars of essays, scaffolds for the essay and other support mechanisms, but there was no support mechanism for students who may have wanted to select the multimodal format. Of course students weren't going to pick the multimodal format, because they had no idea what selecting this format could result in! Needless to say, I modelled a range of formats to all my students, and the more they were exposed to, the more experimental they became. At the time, though, I was a new teacher and kept this a secret, for fear that I would be reprimanded for offering such flexibility in format. I now realise that this is a right for all students.

Jigsaw for interests

Jigsaw is a type of flexible grouping strategy. While a jigsaw can be used to address students' readiness, it can also be incredibly handy when differentiating by students' interests. The jigsaw is also a cooperative learning strategy, allowing students to learn from one another. The first step in a jigsaw is to offer a range of readings that target students' interests. For example, if you think back to the RAFT example of the different symbiotic relationships, I might have had a selection of readings detailing different symbiotic relationships for different animals. I might have asked students to sign up to a particular reading based on what interested them the most. It would not have to be a reading, however; it could be a video to watch, an activity to engage in, or anything that promotes discussion. After students have selected their reading, you place them into home groups. These home groups are made up of students who have selected different readiness. Figure 56 highlights this with the various colours representing the different students and their selection.

Figure 56: Home group as the starting point

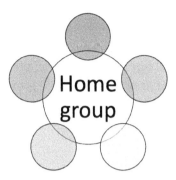

The aim is for students to then move to their expert groups, consisting of students who completed the same reading or activity as one another. As the name suggests, students become experts together in this particular topic. It is here that you may provide further guidance to particular groups, such as more teacher instruction or scaffolding, depending on the make-up of the groups. Students may respond to a series of discussion prompts, perhaps allocating a leader and a scribe to write down key discussion points. The expert group has been represented in Figure 57, where students with the same reading are now grouped together.

Figure 57: Representation of expert groups

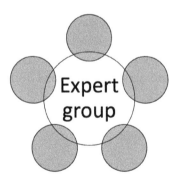

At the completion of the discussion within expert groups, students move back to their original home groups, as shown in Figure 56. Here, they aim to upskill the other group members in the topic or area of interests that they became the expert in. You might provide the group with discussion prompts again, or scaffolds to support discussion. What is great about the jigsaw is that students are given a sense of ownership and freedom, as they are the ones controlling their learning. This gives you the freedom, as the teacher, to provide support to groups or individual students who may require it.

Using the space in Supporting Activity 3 (page 124), consider outlining a jigsaw that addresses students' interests. Outline what the possible readings or activities could be, and any discussion prompts or scaffolds that may be required. Think about the time needed for the groupings and what you will do for groups that may finish earlier than others.

Learning centres

While the jigsaw is effective in allowing students to explore their interests more deeply, I am a firm believer that there are times when students need to be exposed to other students' interests too. Why? Because they may end up developing an interest or passion in something they never thought they would. For a long time, my dad would often make me watch golf with him on the television. I found it incredibly boring, and I dreaded watching it. However, the first time I actually played golf was a different story, because it was not what I had imagined it to be when watching it on TV. Had I not experienced my dad's interest, it would not have become an interest of mine. This is where learning centres can be effective. You may have a series of physical learning centres within the classroom, each targeting a range of students' interests. In those centres are the instructions, materials, directions and relevant assessment materials needed for students to engage in the interest. Students make their way around the learning centres, again being exposed to a range of new interests. A benefit of learning centres is not just that students may learn a new interest, but that they will begin to apply new knowledge and skills to situations and scenarios and become actively engaged in learning.

Co-teaching for interest

Co-teaching is a model of teaching that can enhance a differentiated classroom. Co-teaching is also not specific to just interests and learner preferences; it can be used for differentiation by readiness. Co-teaching does not mean that there are two separate classrooms in which students with lower readiness are always working with the same teacher. Groups must be fluid, and students need to be exposed to a range of peers and teachers. Having inflexible groups – such as students with disabilities with one teacher on one side of the room, and the rest of the students with another teacher on the other side – is not inclusive education. This practice is segregation and goes against the principles of differentiation. Co-teaching, however, has become increasingly recognised as an effective way to provide instruction to diverse students. Similarly, co-teaching allows you to work and learn from colleagues as teachers are paired together to share the responsibilities of planning, instructing and assessing students (CAST, 2023). Scruggs et al. (2007) outlined five models for co-teaching, with Sileo (2011) outlining a sixth model. All of these models for co-teaching are outlined in Figure 58. The reason I have included co-teaching in this chapter is that it can enhance the way you approach differentiation of interests and learner preferences.

Figure 58: Co-teaching models

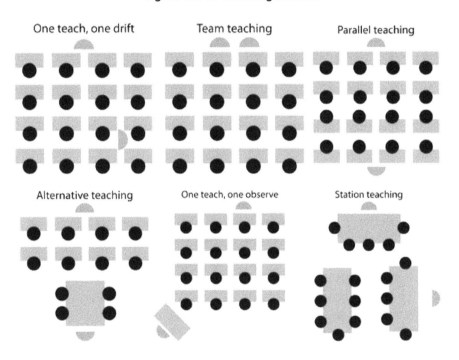

The six methods of co-teaching are:

1. One teach, one float/drift
2. Team teaching
3. Parallel teaching
4. Alternative teaching
5. One teach, one observe
6. Station teaching.

In *one teach, one observe*, one of the teachers can teach the class as a whole, while the other teacher could either be assisting individual students or collecting data on students. This is the perfect way to inform differentiation decisions, as the teacher who is floating or drifting can be determining the readiness levels of students or learning more about their interests or preferences. This same teacher could be taking a proactive approach and beginning to plan future lessons, based on the informal and formal data collected. In *team teaching*, both teachers are delivering the same instruction at the same time. In today's inclusive classrooms, the support/special education/inclusion teacher is often required to work in collaboration with the classroom teacher in order to differentiate to meet the learning needs of all students. In team teaching, you and your colleague are a little like co-presenters. There is no plan for who takes what part of the lesson; you merely work together, jumping in and elaborating as you see fit. This is also a perfect way to provide mentorship to less-experienced teachers or be mentored by someone who may be more experienced in differentiation. When utilising team teaching for differentiation by interest, it could be that students are exposed to a range of interest-based topics, and the teacher who is more passionate about that topic takes more of a lead.

Conclusion and reflection

In this chapter, you have continued your journey of designing differentiated learning experiences through an understanding by design approach – more specifically, exploring differentiation by interest and learner preferences. You have explored learning menus and RAFTs as ways in which you can embed students' interests and learner preferences into your classroom. Similarly, you have studied the importance of differentiated assessment tasks, and how these are necessary for equitable assessment. Lastly, learning centres, jigsaws and co-teaching methods have been added to your repertoire. As we end this chapter, we move away from the steps of dancing in differentiation, per se, moving more towards the role of AI and differentiation, as well as school leaders as enablers in differentiation implementation. Use the space below to reflect on the key learnings from this chapter.

How does the concept of differentiation by interest and learner preferences align with your understanding of differentiation as a whole?

_____

_____

_____

_____

Identify specific strategies from this chapter that resonate with you and your teaching style. What will you adapt to ensure you accommodate interests and learner preferences?

_____

_____

_____

_____

How will you determine what students' interests and learner preferences are?

_____

_____

_____

_____

What are the potential challenges you might face as you begin to incorporate interests and learner preferences more intentionally into your lessons?

_____

_____

_____

_____

_____

Supporting Activity 1

Plan for learning menu

Learning objectives:

K:

U:

D:

Tick choice: ☐ Readiness ☐ Interests ☐ Learner preferences

Main course	Side dishes	Desserts	Beverages

Supporting Activity 2

Planning for a RAFT

Learning objectives:

K:

U:

D:

Pre-assessment to determine students' interests and learner preferences

Role	Audience	Format	Topic

Supporting Activity 3

Plan for jigsaw

CHAPTER 6

Rhythmic innovations

"When you dance to your own rhythm, life taps its toes to your beat."

- TERRI GUILLEMETS

By the end of this chapter:

- Teachers will understand that technology and artificial intelligence offer diverse avenues to differentiate learning experiences.
- Teachers will know that various artificial intelligence tools and platforms exist to facilitate differentiation in the classroom.
- Teachers will be able to evaluate, select and implement appropriate prompts for generative AI, to create learning experiences that address student diversity.
- Teachers will be able to utilise artificial intelligence to design differentiated lesson plans.

In this chapter we will start by exploring the use of generative artificial intelligence in the creation of differentiated lesson plans and/or assessment tasks. I want to preface this chapter by saying that I am not an expert in generative artificial intelligence (AI). I am just someone who has a vested interest in exploring the use of AI in education, particularly the role of AI in inclusive education. I am a firm believer that anything we can use to make differentiation more efficient and effective in our classroom should be harnessed and not feared. If you are interested in deepening your knowledge of AI in education, not just in differentiation, I encourage you to read Leon Furze's new book *Practical AI Strategies*, published by Amba Press. Using AI in your planning and lessons is something I encourage you to embrace – you have been learning to tango and salsa throughout our differentiation journey, but often dances evolve, or new dances come onto the scene, much like techno music became popular in the late eighties and early nineties. Think of AI like a new dance that has arrived on the scene. Techno music helped us to learn new dance moves that we perhaps had not considered or used before. Did techno take away from the dances we had already learned? No. Hence, AI, much like techno, is another dance that can be added to our repertoire and used in our differentiation journey.

I want to emphasise, however, that designing fully differentiated programs and lessons alone should not be done using AI. A certain type of knowledge comes from designing your own learning objectives, assessments and differentiated lessons that you do not acquire from AI. It is like teaching a unit of work that someone else has developed – you never fully know or understand it until you have created it yourself. It is for this reason that

I have not provided you with prompts in generating learning objectives –
I want you to have a firm understanding of what you want your students to
know, understand and be able to do. This also requires knowledge of the
mandated curriculum you are working with.

That being said, AI can provide you with wonderful ideas that you can
implement or adapt for your differentiation, as well as enhancing your
planning (Furze, 2023). For this chapter, you will need access to an
AI chatbot, such as Microsoft Copilot or ChatGPT. I will be using ChatGPT
in my examples. Before you move on, use the space in Supporting Activity
1 (page 143) to reflect on your prior knowledge and use of AI. Perhaps you
have already used AI in other ways? Or perhaps this is the first time you have
heard about AI and ChatGPT? Reflect on your experience with AI and how
you hope to apply it to enhance your teaching practices.

ChatGPT, like other generative AI software, is only as good as what you
enter into it. In this section, you will develop skills in prompt craft, specific
to differentiation. You will be using the *prompt craft* framework developed
by Tom Barrett (Barrett, 2023). According to Barrett (2023), when he asked
ChatGPT to describe what prompt craft is, ChatGPT responded by saying:

> *Prompt crafting refers to the process of creating a specific prompt or set
> of prompts for a language model like GPT to generate text from. It can
> involve carefully selecting words, phrases, and even entire sentences to
> guide the model in a certain direction and produce a desired output.
> This can be used for a variety of applications, such as writing creative
> fiction, generating code, or answering questions.*

You will be exploring ways in which you can create prompts that allow you
to use generative AI to enhance your classroom differentiation. You will be
using the CREATE framework developed by Barrett (2023) to ensure you
create prompts that will get you the desired output. The CREATE framework
is outlined below in Figure 59. Your aim with creating effective prompts will
be to ensure that they are clearly defined and provide enough specificity
to get what you want. For example, asking generative AI to create a tiered
lesson on Year 9 Geography could result in any number of content sets being
provided to you in a lesson. Whereas, providing the learning objectives, as
well as offering suggestions on the flow of your lesson (such as the length of
time, possible resources you want to use, types of grouping you will employ,
and the way you want your lesson to be differentiated), will provide you
with an output that is closer to what you want. Even then, you will want to

include relevant information, such as facts and terminology that you want your students to explore, to be explored in the lesson. You may want some of your lesson dedicated to whole-class instruction, or paired reading, and therefore generative AI will need to know this relevant information for it to be included in the output. In many instances, providing examples of what you are looking for assists AI with the output and increases the clarity. There have been many instances where I have been too vague and ambiguous in my prompts, likely because I was impatient and wanted the answer straight away. I have found that I have been too ambiguous when the output created by AI is not even close to what I have wanted, with AI taking prompts too literally at times. As Barrett (2023) suggests, tinkering with prompts, practising, and evaluating the output will allow you to refine your AI practice. It really is trial and error! But continual exposure is also a factor, given that the landscape of AI is changing so fast – what may work one day, may not the next. As you start to create and refine your prompts, keep track of them. You will save a significant amount of time by copying and pasting prompts rather than typing them out each time.

Figure 59: CREATE Framework by Barrett (2023)

Clarity	• Clearly define the task or intent of the prompt, including specific information about the output.
Relevant information	• Provide relevant details, including specific keywords and facts, the tone, audience, format and structure.
Examples	• Use examples in the prompt to provide context and direction for the output.
Avoid ambiguity	• Focus on the key information and delete unnecessary details in the prompt.
Tinker	• Test and refine the prompt through multiple iterations. Explore different input versions to discover best results.
Evaluate	• Continuously evaluate the output and adjust the prompt as needed to improve the quality.

Let's use the CREATE framework to start designing your first prompt for Generative AI. I have included my Year 10 Science learning objectives from Chapter 2, as you will use these as part of your prompting. Figure 60 re-outlines these learning objectives. In Figure 61, I have guided you by providing some sample prompts that you can build upon. These prompts are a starting point for you and are by no means perfect. You will need to utilise the CREATE framework to adapt these prompts. However, if you are confident in the use of AI and feel you are of high readiness, you do not need to use my possible prompts.

Figure 60: Tom's learning objectives

Students will understand that:
- Heredity and genetic diversity are determined by a series of actions.
- Scientific theories are a way of explaining the world.
- The past has shaped the diversity in the world.

Students will know:
- How the theory of natural selection can explain evolution
- How natural selection contributes to diversity in populations.

Students will be able to:
- Use scientific theories
- Explain the impact of the past and present on diversity
- Analyse scientific evidence.

Figure 61: Possible prompts specific to differentiation

Possible prompts for generative AI and differentiation
- Create a pre-assessment that I can use to gauge my students' understanding of the following learning objectives <copy/paste learning objectives> and suggest ways that I can pre-assess their knowledge. Create criteria for readiness tiers and who will go into each of the three tiers (high readiness, middle readiness, and lower readiness) based on the pre-assessment and create the pre-assessment questions or activity.
- Create a tiered lesson with <insert number of tiers> tiers using the following learning objectives <copy/paste learning objectives> based on student readiness. Ensure the lesson has an introduction and a check for understanding of the learning objectives at the conclusion of the lesson.
- Using the following learning objectives <copy/paste learning objectives> for the lesson and using the following student interests <copy/paste students' interests>, generate a lesson plan that allows all students to meet the learning objectives, but students can select the task or activity that corresponds to their interests.
- Using the following learning objectives <copy/paste learning objectives>, generate an assessment using the following student interests <copy/

paste students' interests>, and assess students on the following achievement standards <copy/paste achievement standard(s)>.

- Using the following learning objectives <copy/paste learning objectives>, create a RAFT with at least four different options for students. A RAFT is a differentiated task where students select a Role, Audience, Format and Topic. All options need to allow students to meet the learning objectives, no matter the choice.

- Using this existing lesson plan/assessment task <copy/paste lesson plan or assessment task>, how can I differentiate to suit students' readiness levels or learner preferences <insert learner preferences>?

- Suggest resources or materials that I can use in this existing lesson plan/assessment task <copy/paste lesson plan/assessment task> that can cater to various readiness levels and explain how they will support differentiated learning.

- Generate an assessment task that offers options for students to demonstrate what they know, understand and can do in relation to the learning objectives <copy/paste learning objectives> and the achievement standards <copy/paste relevant achievement standard(s)>.

- Using this lesson plan <copy/paste lesson plan>, how can I include methods for tracking student progress against the learning objectives?

- Using this lesson plan <copy/paste lesson plan>, how can I utilise flexible grouping strategies that cater for different readiness levels but still allow all students to meet the same learning objectives?

- Generate a task sheet and rubric based on the following <Insert achievement standards>.

Using the learning objectives above, or your own learning objectives created earlier in the book, use ChatGPT or another generative AI program to create a pre-assessment task for your students to complete, so you can gauge their knowledge, understanding and skills against those learning objectives. Make a note, in Supporting Activity 2 (page 143), of the prompt you have used. For example, I asked ChatGPT:

Create a pre-assessment that I can use to gauge my students' understanding of the following learning objectives <I inserted the above learning objectives> and suggest ways that I can pre-assess their knowledge. Create criteria for readiness tiers and who will go into each of the three tiers (high readiness, middle readiness, and lower readiness) based on the pre-assessment.

When I first entered this into ChatGPT, I expected an activity or task, perhaps with a series of questions I could give to my students to gauge their readiness levels. However, I was presented with the output shown in Figure 62. I was not specific enough, and according to the CREATE framework, my prompt had too much ambiguity. As you can see, ChatGPT did not actually create the pre-assessment; it only gave me some suggestions on what I could do. That being said, some of the suggestions would prove very useful as a pre-assessment; however, I would need to create the questions or actual task myself, given that I was only presented with ideas. A positive aspect of this prompt is that it allows you to have set criteria for who enters each tier. Where people often go wrong is that they design fantastic pre-assessments but assume that the number of questions answered correctly correlates with the readiness level. For example, answering nine out of ten correctly means that the student is of high readiness, compared to a student who received, say, four out of ten. While not absolutely wrong, you need to look deeper at what the questions are trying to elicit from students. Two students could receive five out of ten but answer completely different questions correctly, therefore having different levels of readiness. For this reason, keeping pre-assessments short and concise is best.

Figure 62: Result from prompt input into ChatGPT

To assess your students' understanding of the learning objectives you've outlined, you can design a pre-assessment that incorporates various question formats and activities. Here's a suggestion for the pre-assessment along with readiness tier criteria:

Pre-Assessment

Part 1: Multiple Choice and Short Answer Questions

1. *Heredity and Genetic Diversity*
    - Multiple-choice questions assessing understanding of heredity, genetic diversity, and their determinants.
    - Short answer questions requiring explanations of genetic concepts.

2. *Scientific Theories*
    - Multiple-choice questions on the nature and purpose of scientific theories.
    - Short answer questions explaining the role of scientific theories in understanding the world.

3. *Impact of the Past on Diversity*
   - Multiple-choice questions exploring the influence of historical events on diversity.
   - Short answer questions connecting past events to current diversity.

Part 2: Scenario Analysis

Provide a scenario where students have to apply the theory of natural selection to explain changes in a population over time. Ask them to analyse the scenario and provide explanations using the theory.

Part 3: Evidence Analysis

Present scientific evidence (such as graphs, charts, or a case study) related to natural selection and diversity. Ask students to analyse the evidence and draw conclusions about how natural selection contributes to diversity.

Readiness Tier Criteria

High Readiness

Students demonstrating high readiness typically:

- Provide comprehensive and accurate explanations of heredity, genetic diversity, and their determinants.
- Show a deep understanding of scientific theories and their application.
- Effectively apply the theory of natural selection to explain scenarios and analyse evidence to draw nuanced conclusions about diversity.

Middle Readiness

Students showing middle readiness typically:

- Show a reasonable understanding of heredity, genetic diversity, and scientific theories, though with occasional gaps in knowledge or understanding.
- Can apply the theory of natural selection to some extent, but may struggle with more complex scenarios or evidence analysis.

Lower Readiness

Students with lower readiness may:

- Display limited understanding of heredity, genetic diversity, or scientific theories.
- Struggle to apply the theory of natural selection or analyse scientific evidence effectively.
- Demonstrate significant gaps in knowledge or misunderstanding of core concepts.

Evaluate and classify students into these tiers based on their performance in the various sections of the pre-assessment. This classification can guide your teaching approach, allowing you to tailor instruction to address specific gaps in understanding.

The second time around, I used the same prompt again, but I asked ChatGPT to create the pre-assessment questions. Figure 63 highlights the revised answer from ChatGPT. This time, ChatGPT provided me with some possible questions I could ask my students; furthermore, ChatGPT organised these into three different areas. Effectively, I could either focus my lesson on all three aspects – heredity and genetic diversity, scientific theories, and the impact of the past on diversity – or I could create three different lessons and administer one of these at a time. If my students had varying levels of readiness for heredity, genetic diversity and scientific theories, I would likely focus on one of these per lesson. This is where you have to be flexible and prepared to adapt what you teach and when you teach it, based on the data from the pre-assessments. This responsive approach is a real hallmark of differentiation (Tomlinson & Borland, 2022).

Figure 63: Second output from ChatGPT

Part 1: Multiple Choice and Short Answer Questions
Heredity and Genetic Diversity

1. *Multiple Choice*

   Which of the following best defines heredity?

   A) The passing of physical traits from parents to offspring.
   B) The study of genetic mutations.
   C) The influence of the environment on an organism's traits.
   D) The process of natural selection.

2. *Short Answer*

   Explain the difference between genotype and phenotype and provide an example of each.

Scientific Theories

3. *Multiple Choice*

   What is the primary purpose of a scientific theory?

   A) To describe observations.
   B) To propose a guess about natural phenomena.
   C) To provide an explanation based on evidence.
   D) To establish laws of nature.

4. *Short Answer*

   Describe how a scientific theory differs from a scientific hypothesis.

Impact of the Past on Diversity

5. *Multiple Choice*

   Which of the following historical events could have a significant impact on the diversity of species today?

   A) Ice Age
   B) Industrial Revolution
   C) Invention of the internet
   D) Space exploration era

6. *Short Answer*

   Provide an example of how a past environmental change could have influenced the diversity of species in a particular region.

Given that you have seen an example of some prompts, as well as the refinement of prompts using ChatGPT, you should now complete Supporting Activity 3 (page 143), outlining the changes you made to your original prompt. Were you more specific this time? Or did you perhaps add further instructions to add greater clarity to what you were asking? Look back at the CREATE model and reflect on what was useful in allowing you to elicit a better output from AI.

The key with AI is to have fun and play around with it. Like many educational resources and technology, AI is just one tool. Do not just take what it says and slap it into a generic lesson – you are still the expert teacher, not the AI. However, use AI to enhance the way you approach a differentiated classroom. As you further play with AI, consider the questions by Barrett (2023) that you can ask yourself to ensure that your prompts align with the CREATE framework (Figure 64). Look back at your original prompt and ask yourself these questions, refining as you see fit.

Figure 64: Questions to ask yourself with designing prompts

When reviewing **clarity**, ask yourself:
1. Is the task or intent of the prompt clear?
2. Are all required information and parameters included in the prompt?
3. Have I described a distinct chunk of what I want to create?

When reviewing **relevant information**, ask yourself:

1. Have I included all the information about this?
2. Are the audience, format and tone described clearly?
3. What facts and details do I need to reference?

When reviewing **examples**, ask yourself:
1. Which part of this can I provide as an example?
2. What templates and exemplars have I used in the past?
3. Have I included a clear example of what I am trying to create?

When reviewing **ambiguity**, ask yourself:
1. What can I delete?
2. Which part of the prompt is a little ambiguous?
3. Have I edited my prompt for clarity and removed unnecessary words?

When reviewing **tinker**, ask yourself:
1. Which version is closest to what I want?
2. How can I edit the prompt to emphasise different aspects?
3. Can I tinker with the prompt by offering more exemplar direction?

When reviewing **evaluate**, ask yourself:
1. How close is this to what I want?
2. Who can I share this output with to get a new perspective?
3. Which other AI tools can I use to generate some different outputs?

While you have been using prompts to create lessons with AI, AI can also be used to create specific types of tasks and assessments. For example, you have already explored the creation of a RAFT to address students' interests or learner preferences. AI can help you to create the RAFT. I entered the prompt in Figure 65 into ChatGPT and was given the RAFT output (Figure 66). To make this even more specific, I could have pre-assessed my students' interests and/or learner preferences and entered these into my prompt, to ensure the RAFT was utilising their interests and learner preferences. At the moment, the RAFT has a range of learner preferences and the different options *may* be of interest to students; however, as I did not pre-assess, this is not quite differentiation. A strength of this RAFT, however, is that no matter the choice students make, they are all working towards the same learning objectives; thus no-one is disadvantaged. I could go even further here, asking AI to create task sheets for each of the options, or even to suggest particular resources that students could use for these options. For students who have selected an option but whom you know have lower readiness levels, you may even ask AI to generate a scaffold for their option.

Similarly, I could paste in the relevant achievement standards, asking AI to create a rubric that could be used for summative assessment.

Figure 65: Prompt for RAFT generation by AI

Using the following learning objectives <Students will understand that: • heredity and genetic diversity are determined by a series of actions • scientific theories are a way of explaining the world. • the past has shaped the diversity in the world. Students will know: • How the theory of natural selection can explain evolution • How natural selection contributes to diversity in populations Students will be able to: • Use scientific theories • Explain the impact of the past and present on diversity • Analyse scientific evidence> create a RAFT with at least four different options for students. A RAFT is a differentiated task where students select a Role, Audience, Format and Topic. All options need to allow students to meet the learning objectives, no matter the choice.

Figure 66: AI RAFT generation

Option 1

Role: Genetic Researcher
Audience: Fellow Scientists
Format: Research Paper
Topic: Explaining the Role of Genetic Sequencing in Determining Heredity and Genetic Diversity

Task Description: As a genetic researcher, your task is to write a research paper that delves into the methods and importance of genetic sequencing in understanding heredity and genetic diversity. Explain how specific actions at the genetic level determine these traits. Discuss the implications of this understanding for future scientific endeavours.

Option 2

Role: Science Communicator
Audience: General Public
Format: Infographic
Topic: The Influence of Past Events on Present Biodiversity

Task Description: Your role is to create an informative infographic aimed at the general public. Explain how historical events have shaped the current diversity of life on Earth. Use visuals and concise explanations to illustrate the impact of the past on present biodiversity.

Option 3

Role: Natural Selection Advocate
Audience: High School Biology Students
Format: Classroom Presentation
Topic: How Natural Selection Drives Evolutionary Changes

Task Description: Assume the role of a natural selection advocate. Create a classroom presentation aimed at high school biology students. Explain in simple terms how natural selection operates and its contribution to the evolution of species. Use clear examples and visuals to enhance understanding.

Option 4

Role: Scientific Journalist
Audience: Readers of a Science Magazine
Format: News Article
Topic: Analysing Recent Scientific Evidence on Natural Selection and Population Diversity

Task Description: As a scientific journalist, your task is to write a news article for a science magazine. Analyse recent scientific studies or evidence related to natural selection and its impact on population diversity. Present the findings in an engaging and accessible manner for the magazine's readership.

These differentiated RAFT options provide students with diverse tasks while allowing them to engage with the learning objectives, catering to various strengths and preferences. Each option encourages students to apply their understanding of heredity, scientific theories, the impact of the past on diversity, natural selection, and scientific evidence analysis.

Using the space in Supporting Activity 4 (page 144), write out your prompt to create either a RAFT or another differentiated lesson plan/activity/task. Write your original prompt first and then enter this into the AI. After the AI has generated the outcome, reflect on what was generated and revisit the CREATE questions to ask yourself, tinkering with the prompt and re-writing it again in the space provided. Reflect upon what you did differently when you entered the revised prompt.

It is important to remember that AI does not need to be used to *reinvent the wheel* – that is to say, if you already have existing work/tasks/lesson plans/activities that perhaps need updating, AI can help do this too.

As Leon Furze calls it – *refreshing* (Furze, 2023). Much like Tom Barrett, Leon outlines the importance of creating quality prompts. For this example, I decided to refresh a lesson plan that I completed close to 10 years ago (Figure 67), which was not very good! I think at the time I likely thought I was differentiating, because I made some changes to the standard lesson, but looking back, it was not really differentiated because I did not know what I was differentiating *for*. (Readiness? Interests? Learner preferences?) Hence, it was not differentiation, because it was not purposeful. Even my learning objectives were not the best. However, like I said, differentiation is a dance, and it takes practice! I have provided a snippet of the original lesson, which was starting to introduce students to the difference between quantitative and qualitative analysis, in the context of Psychology. This snippet allows me to show you how AI can refresh old lessons. Figure 68 shows the refreshed lesson using AI.

Figure 67: Year 11 Psychology lesson snippet

Learning objectives

- Students will know the difference between qualitative and quantitative research methods.
- Students will be able to analyse qualitative and quantitative data in the area of psychology.
- Students will understand that data can be represented in a variety of ways and classified as quantitative or qualitative.

Types of data

- Scientists collect two different types of data: qualitative data and quantitative data.
- Qualitative data are descriptions in words of what is being observed. They are based on some quality of an observation, such as colour, odour or texture.
- Quantitative data are numeric measurements. The data are objective – they are the same no matter who measures them. They include measurements such as mass, volume, temperature, distance, concentration, time, or frequency.

Example

Suppose a marine biologist observes the behaviour and activities of dolphins. She identifies different dolphins within the group and observes them every day for a month. She records detailed observations about their behaviours. Some of her observations are qualitative data and some are quantitative data.

Ask students as a class to outline what they think the difference between qualitative and quantitative data is.

Qualitative data examples

- Dolphin colours range from grey to white.
- Dolphins in a pod engage in play behaviour.
- Dolphins have smooth skin.

Quantitative data examples

- There are nine dolphins in this pod.
- Dolphins eat the equivalent of 4–5% of their body mass each day.
- The sonar frequency most often used by the dolphins is around 100 kHz.

Notice that the qualitative data are descriptions. The quantitative data are objective, numerical measurements.

Activity

Qualitative vs. quantitative

Identify data types

Suppose that you are a biologist studying elephants in their natural habitat in Africa. You observe their behaviours and interaction and take photographs of their interactions to study later. Examine the photograph of the elephants shown above.

1. Give two examples of qualitative data that could be obtained from the photograph of the elephants.
2. Give two examples of quantitative data that could be obtained from the photograph of the elephants.

Figure 68: **Refreshed** *lesson using ChatGPT*

Lesson prompt

Using this existing lesson plan/assessment task <insert lesson plan>, how can I differentiate to suit students' readiness levels? Suggest resources or materials for each of the tiers and other activities. Make sure all tiers have the opportunity to meet the same learning objectives. Write each tier out as a lesson plan.

High Readiness Tier

- **Resources/Materials:** Scientific Journals: Provide access to advanced articles discussing research methodologies and data analysis in psychology, emphasising advanced qualitative and quantitative approaches.
- **Case Studies:** Offer complex case studies with detailed qualitative and quantitative data sets in psychology for high readiness students to analyse.
- **Data Analysis Software:** Introduce advanced statistical software for data analysis, allowing students to explore complex datasets.

Activities:

- **Case Study Analysis:** Engage students in analysing sophisticated case studies employing both qualitative and quantitative data. Encourage discussions on data interpretations and methodological choices.
- **Advanced Data Analysis Project:** Assign a research project requiring high readiness students to collect and analyse their own qualitative and quantitative data in psychology. Emphasize representation and interpretation methods.

Middle Readiness Tier

- **Resources/Materials:** Simplified Readings: Provide simplified readings explaining the differences between qualitative and quantitative research methods in psychology.
- **Structured Data Sets:** Offer structured and manageable data sets with examples of both qualitative and quantitative data in psychology.
- **Visual Aids:** Use simplified visual aids to illustrate different ways of representing qualitative and quantitative data.

Activities:

- **Guided Data Analysis:** Guide students through analysing structured data sets, prompting discussions on how to differentiate between qualitative and quantitative data in psychology.

- **Group Discussions:** Organize group discussions using visual aids to identify diverse representations of qualitative and quantitative data in psychology, encouraging peer learning.

Low Readiness Tier

- **Resources/Materials:** Simple Explanatory Materials: Provide simplified explanations using visuals or storybooks to introduce the concepts of qualitative and quantitative data in psychology.
- **Picture Cards:** Use picture cards depicting basic examples of qualitative and quantitative data in psychology.
- **Basic Visual Supports:** Use basic visual supports such as charts or graphs showing simple representations of data.

Activities:

- **Interactive Storytelling:** Engage students in an interactive storytelling session using visuals or picture cards to identify and differentiate between qualitative and quantitative data in psychology.
- **Matching Activities:** Create matching activities where students match basic examples of qualitative and quantitative data in psychology with corresponding visuals or descriptions.

Let's unpack the refreshed lesson a little more. A significant strength is that AI has generated a variety of ways that the lesson could be differentiated. In fact, there are opportunities to differentiate content, process and product in this output from AI. For example, varying materials could be offered in a range of complexities to differentiate by content. The higher readiness tier could look at scientific peer-reviewed articles, while the lower readiness tier could be provided with a variety of visual datasets for both qualitative and quantitative data; hence there would be various levels of complexity in the texts provided to students. There is an emphasis in all tiers on using visuals and a variety of activities suggested for each tier. In fact, I would not utilise all of these in the one lesson, as the lesson could quickly become overwhelming for both you as the teacher and your students. You might simply adapt the complexity of the texts provided to each readiness tier, focusing on content with more complex terminology, or using the visual supports. While AI could be used to go even further, helping you create scaffolds etc., doing this yourself allows you to really understand the needs of your learners and to be clear about how you are differentiating for them. Using AI to refresh a lesson offers you a different perspective and a set of ideas to make differentiation more efficient and effective.

Chapter summary

AI is constantly changing and evolving. Therefore, you must be prepared to engage in the process of continuous learning with AI, to ensure that you use it to its full capabilities and that its use can be purposeful as you navigate the differentiated classroom. You have explored the importance of prompts when using AI, and how prompts need to be refined and tinkered with to achieve the desired outcome. Furthermore, you have looked at a variety of examples of outputs from AI and seen how these outputs can be used to differentiate more efficiently and effectively. AI is an exciting space to play in, as it is always changing and allows you to create a contemporary classroom that harnesses the benefits of such technologies.

Supporting Activity 1

Reflection on your use of AI.

Supporting Activity 2

Prompt for creation of pre-assessment for learning objectives.

Supporting Activity 3

What changes did you make to your prompt to improve it? Reflect on the CREATE model.

Supporting Activity 4

Original and revised prompt for differentiated RAFT/task/activity/lesson.

Reflect on the changes made between the original prompt and the revised prompt.

CHAPTER 7

Stepping into confidence

"Mistakes are proof that you are trying."

- JENNIFER LIM

Learning objectives

By the end of this chapter:

- Teachers will understand that attitudes and self-efficacy significantly impact the implementation of differentiation, influencing instructional choices and approaches to meeting student diversity.
- Teachers will be able to assess their own attitudes towards differentiation and self-efficacy in catering to diverse learners, identifying areas of strength and areas needing improvement.
- Teachers will know the various professional development methods that can be utilised to support differentiation implementation.
- Teachers will be able to plan to collaborate with colleagues to develop and implement strategies that embed differentiation.

This chapter aims to help you understand teacher attitudes and self-efficacy. Both of these play a crucial role in understanding how to become more inclusive and may guide you in how you approach differentiation in your classroom. Furthermore, gaining a deeper understanding of attitudes and self-efficacy will assist you and your school in implementing relevant professional development and supports, to help teachers become more efficacious in utilising differentiation, as well as helping to shape more positive attitudes towards inclusion, diversity and differentiation.

Attitudes are essential elements in professional competence and a predictor of how successfully an inclusive school system is implemented (Börnert-Ringleb et al., 2020). Given that they are a predictor, you need to know how to acknowledge your own attitudes towards inclusion and differentiation, and how to help your colleagues acknowledge theirs, to either harness this positivity or find ways to assist your colleagues in adapting their attitude. According to Eagly and Chaiken (1998), attitudes can be divided into three components: (A) affective, (B) behaviour and (C) cognitive. Figure 69 provides an example of how the ABC model may work in the context of differentiation. As you can see, I have highlighted an example of what you might see if a teacher has a negative attitude towards differentiation. Using this model allows you to acknowledge the attitudes you hold towards differentiation and/or inclusion. Use the space in Supporting Activity 1 (page 164) to acknowledge your attitude towards differentiation and inclusion. Being aware of your attitude will allow you to have greater insight into the way you think, and how that thinking affects your behaviour, particularly towards differentiation.

Figure 69: Affective, behaviour, cognitive (ABC) model

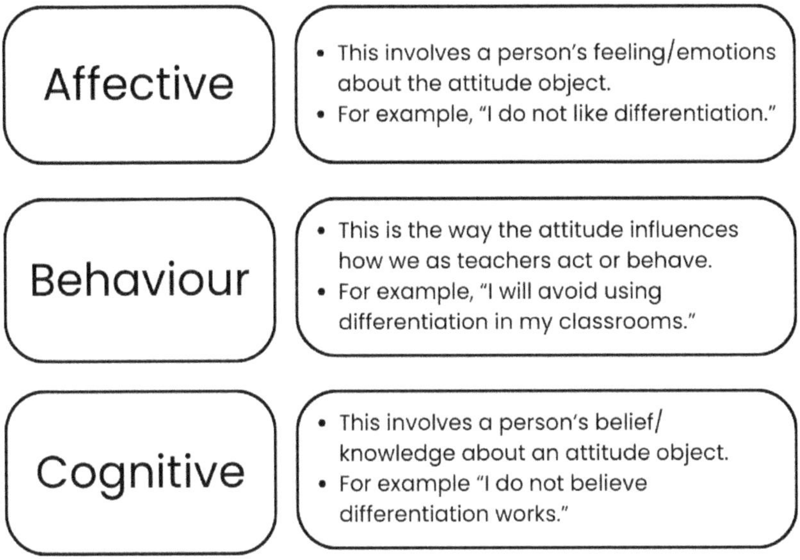

Affective	• This involves a person's feeling/emotions about the attitude object. • For example, "I do not like differentiation."
Behaviour	• This is the way the attitude influences how we as teachers act or behave. • For example, "I will avoid using differentiation in my classrooms."
Cognitive	• This involves a person's belief/knowledge about an attitude object. • For example "I do not believe differentiation works."

In contrast to attitudes, self-efficacy is a teacher's belief in their ability to carry out effective teaching practices, and in the context of this book it is a teacher's belief in their ability to carry out practices for diverse classrooms (Monteiro et al., 2019; San Martin et al., 2021). Albert Bandura, a prominent researcher in self-efficacy, identifies four sources of self-efficacy (Bandura, 1997):

1. Mastery experiences
2. Vicarious experiences
3. Verbal and social persuasion
4. Psychological or affective states.

Bandura (1997) proposes that *mastery experiences* are the most powerful, in that when a person completes a task and evaluates their efforts as having been successful, their self-efficacy increases. In the context of differentiation, this can mean that applying differentiation practices in your classroom and seeing success in such application is likely to increase your self-efficacy. This point highlights what I have been reiterating throughout this book. Putting into practice what you have been learning and sticking it out to become more confident in such differentiation practices has the greatest impact. I will discuss this in more detail later in this chapter, along with methods of professional development that you can apply yourself and with your colleagues to develop mastery experiences in differentiation.

In contrast, Bandura's *vicarious experiences* are developed by observation of others. As you watch others, you gauge an understanding of your own capabilities. Hence, observing other teachers engaging in differentiation implementation in their classrooms may help you to develop greater self-efficacy in differentiation. Sharing good practice with one another can have a profound effect, as you will be able to add new differentiation tools to your repertoire that perhaps you had not previously considered. *Verbal and social persuasion* is the third source of self-efficacy, relating to when you receive encouragement and evaluative feedback from people such as peers and colleagues. In the context of differentiation, this corresponds with colleagues providing feedback to each other on the effectiveness of their differentiation implementation, as well as celebrating successes in differentiation. Lastly, self-efficacy can be developed and influenced by your *psychological or affective state*, which is linked to the impact of one's mood, anxiety and stress. For example, anxiety towards differentiation may be a barrier to developing self-efficacy in differentiation.

You can see in Figure 70 that each of these four sources plays a role in helping you and your colleagues develop self-efficacy and implementation (behaviour) in differentiation.

Figure 70: Bandura's self-efficacy

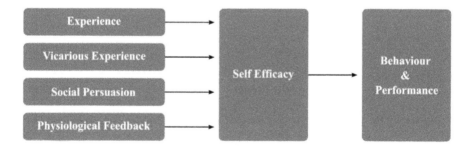

Using Supporting Activity 2 (page 164), which has the four sources of self-efficacy based on Bandura, outline your experience in each of these areas. For example, were there times when you trialled a teaching practice or method in your classroom that you saw success in? Perhaps you can recall a time when you observed a colleague and took what they were doing and implemented this into your own classroom. Or perhaps you have not had the opportunity to observe colleagues or receive feedback from others. Reflect on these situations and experiences in the activity.

There is a connection between attitudes and self-efficacy – whereby having a positive attitude allows you to trial and experiment with differentiation, further contributing to a sense of self-efficacy. This is why you may have to move out of your comfort zone in relation to ways in which you may have been teaching for a number of years. You have reflected in Chapter 1 on your use of differentiation and inclusive practices and just now on your attitudes and self-efficacy. As you look back at these, I want you to think about what it would take for you to develop a more positive attitude towards differentiation and inclusion and/or greater self-efficacy. What could you do, or what could your school do to support you in this? Use the space in Supporting Activity 3 (page 165) to document your thoughts. You will revisit these as you start to explore different forms of professional development that can support your and your colleagues' differentiation journey.

As you have been progressing through this book, you have explored how you can use differentiation in your classroom context. You have also explored the importance of developing a positive attitude towards inclusion and differentiation, as well as the importance of developing greater self-efficacy in implementing differentiation. As you move through this chapter, you will explore some of the various modes of professional development that can assist you and your colleagues in developing your skills in differentiation and becoming more efficacious and positive in this area.

Figure 71 provides a brief overview of some of the ways that schools and leaders can upskill and benefit from professional development in relation to differentiation, encouraging staff to develop relevant knowledge and practical skills. Try not to look at these as siloed approaches – a combined approach will only strengthen differentiation. Sharp et al. (2018) synthesised key research in the area of professional development and have identified six characteristics of high-quality professional development. These are found when:

1. Teacher learning occurs over extended periods.
2. Content is specific and practical.
3. Content is delivered by those with expert knowledge.
4. Teacher learning is connected to student learning.

5. Teachers learn together in communities of practice in their own work contexts.
6. Professional development is well supported by school leaders.

Each of the four modes of professional development shown in Figure 70 allows for some or all of the elements of high-quality professional development to be met.

Figure 71: Outline of ways schools and leaders can facilitate differentiation

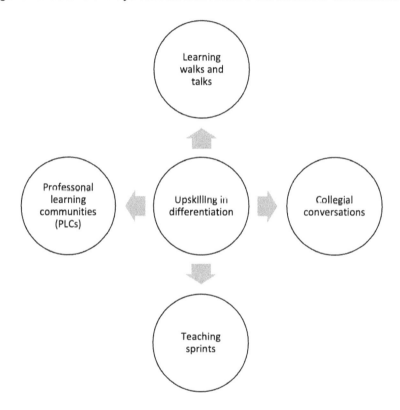

Learning walks and talks

Learning walks (Fisher & Frey, 2014) and learning walks and talks (Sharratt, 2018) have been shown to improve teachers' instructional practices and can be used as a method for teachers to highlight the various differentiated practices they feel they do well, during classroom visits by other teachers. Research has shown that learning walks can create a more collaborative culture and increase reflective dialogue and the sharing of instructional practices (Allen & Topolka-Jorissen, 2014). Classroom teachers act as observers, with the aim of gaining a comprehensive picture of current practices in differentiation in others' classrooms (Allen & Topolka-Jorissen, 2014).

There are three types of learning walks, as outlined by James-Ward et al. (2013) in Figure 72. You and your colleagues could undertake ghost walks, where you walk through a series of empty classrooms, with no students present. There is no instruction to evaluate; instead, you discuss the physical classroom environment. You might look for evidence of quality learning objectives being conveyed in the classroom, or students' work being displayed.

Secondly, you and your colleagues could engage in capacity-building learning walks, with the aim of gathering evidence – in this case, on effective differentiation practices. Like ghost walks, these are typically short in duration. Both ghost walks and capacity-building learning walks could be done with a partner or a small group and organised during non-teaching time, or you could negotiate with school administrators to give you and your colleagues an hour to conduct the walk.

Lastly, you and your faculty could engage in faculty learning walks, which typically last all day. The aim here is to engage as a faculty to visit a range of classrooms across the school in varying subjects on a particular area. In the case of differentiation, you may want to simply observe teachers' differentiation practices, or you could look more deeply at a particular aspect, such as differentiation by readiness, or how teachers use flexible grouping strategies.

Figure 72: Types of learning walks (James-Ward et al., 2013)

Type of walk	Purpose	Time	Participants	Follow-up after the walk
Ghost walk	To examine classrooms without students present.	1 hour	Principal, assistant principal, teachers, building leadership team, coaches, and professional learning community.	Summary of data collected: evidence and wondering processed with entire faculty.

Type of walk	Purpose	Time	Participants	Follow-up after the walk
Capacity-building learning walks	To collect data, looking for evidence of the implementation of effective practices and gaining insights into next steps.	1 hour	Principal, assistant principal, coaches, and other members of the building leadership team.	Summary of data collected: evidence and wonderings processed with entire faculty.
Faculty learning walks	To involve the entire faculty in visiting classrooms.	All day during planning periods	Principal, assistant principal, and whoever is available each period of time segment, ultimately involving the entire faculty throughout the year.	Summary of data collected: evidence and wonderings processed with entire faculty.

While there are different types of learning walks that you and your colleagues can take, there is a general outline to these walks that can be followed (Figure 73). Learning walks shouldn't just be walking in and out of classrooms. There needs to be reflective conversation led by a facilitator, asking participants what they noticed, what surprised them, and what the classrooms had in common with their own practice. There needs to be a view forward, looking at what the observers might now do in their own classrooms. The debrief is a crucial part of the learning walk process.

Understanding where you and the group are at in your journey of differentiation will determine how your learning walk is approached. For example, teachers who have lower readiness and confidence in utilising differentiation, or do not yet have much understanding of differentiation as a philosophy, might consider observing teachers who are differentiating well across the school. Put a call out to teachers asking if any of them are using differentiation in the classroom and would be willing to have staff members come and observe their classrooms. Similarly, while exploring differentiation may be the focus, go and observe a range of classrooms, as you may be able to pick up on differentiation practices being utilised in different ways.

Figure 73: Outline of learning walk

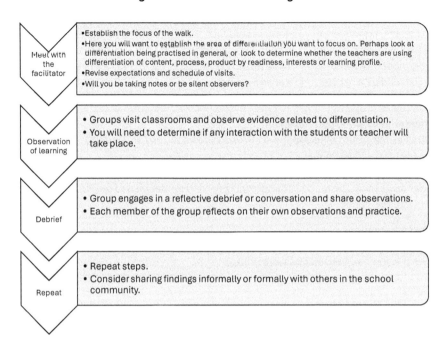

Meet with the facilitator
- Establish the focus of the walk.
- Here you will want to establish the area of differentiation you want to focus on. Perhaps look at differentiation being practised in general, or look to determine whether the teachers are using differentiation of content, process, product by readiness, interests or learning profile.
- Revise expectations and schedule of visits.
- Will you be taking notes or be silent observers?

Observation of learning
- Groups visit classrooms and observe evidence related to differentiation.
- You will need to determine if any interaction with the students or teacher will take place.

Debrief
- Group engages in a reflective debrief or conversation and share observations.
- Each member of the group reflects on their own observations and practice.

Repeat
- Repeat steps.
- Consider sharing findings informally or formally with others in the school community.

Learning walks can be done in small or large groups and may involve you being the observed, rather than the observer. In fact, highlighting differentiation practices that you are confident in will only influence others to try the same. Consider using the following template (Figure 74) to guide your observations as you conduct a learning walk. This template allows you to connect to the various elements of differentiation. Use the prompt questions as a guide.

Figure 74: Template for learning walks in differentiation

Differentiation of content	Differentiation of process	Differentiation of product
What evidence suggests the teacher is differentiating by content? Has the complexity of content been adapted for students?	What evidence suggests the teacher is differentiating by process?	What evidence suggests the teacher is differentiating by product?

Readiness	Interests	Learner preferences
How do you know the teacher has differentiated by readiness? What is the teacher doing? What are the students doing?	How are students' interests being utilised in the lesson? What are students doing?	Are students able to demonstrate their learning in a variety of ways?

Differentiation principles observed
- Are flexible groups employed? If so, how do you know they are flexible?
- Is the teacher "teaching up"?
- Has the teacher drawn their learning objectives from the curriculum?
- Has the teacher shown proactive planning for differentiation and responsiveness towards students?

Other observations
- Were learning objectives clear and evident to students?
- What instructional strategies were utilised?

Debrief
Discuss the above elements – what are some of the key takeaways? What are your next steps? What feedback will you give the teachers who participated? (Strengths? Suggestions for improvement?)

You might also consider the following checklist in your decisions (Figure 75). This is not an exhaustive guide but allows you to make quick ticks on what you have observed regarding differentiation. Consider adapting to your context. Remember, you may not observe all of these aspects in a lesson, as it depends on how the teacher is differentiating. For example, if a teacher is differentiating by readiness, you may not see interest-based learning centres that lesson. Keep this in mind when observing.

Figure 75: Checklist for learning walks

- ☐ Lesson utilises learning objectives in the form of know, understand and do.
- ☐ All students are working towards the same learning objectives.
- ☐ Teacher utilises flexible grouping strategies to facilitate interest, readiness or learner preferences.
- ☐ Teacher is differentiating according to readiness, interests and/or learner preferences.
- ☐ There is clear evidence of differentiation by either content, process or product (or a combination).

☐ There is evidence of assessment used to guide the teacher's differentiation decisions (formative, summative and/or pre-assessment).

☐ The teacher has utilised a variety of materials and resources, depending on the differentiation employed.

☐ The teacher has utilised a range of strategies to provide feedback to students.

☐ Differentiated tasks/activities are evident, such as RAFTs, learning menus, or other appropriately designed tasks.

Collegial conversations

Now, more than ever, teachers are time-poor and are being asked to do much more in the face of the current teacher shortage in Australia (Australian Government, 2023a). Having looked at the work of Bandura (1997) earlier, you know that verbal and social persuasion influences one's self-efficacy. Therefore, having conversations with colleagues regarding differentiation implementation, including successes and challenges, is crucial in developing your own self-efficacy. Collegial conversations encourage critical reflection on practice, allowing you, as the teacher, to become a learner yourself (Selkrig & Keamy, 2015). While collegial conversations may be formal or informal, informal conversations may not result in a deep enough or critical reflection (Selkrig & Keamy, 2015). Figure 76 highlights some guiding questions that you may want to use to support collegial conversations in an informal way, such as at faculty meetings, during staff room conversations, etc.

Figure 76: Example of guiding questions to support collegial conversations

1. How do you currently recognise and address the diversity that exists in your classroom?
2. What differentiation strategies have you found effective in addressing diversity in your classroom?
3. How do you determine students' readiness levels, interests and learner preferences and what have you found most and least effective?
4. How are you using flexible grouping in your classroom? What advice would you give someone who has not used flexible grouping strategies before?
5. What obstacles or challenges have you encountered when attempting to implement differentiation strategies?

Collegial conversations can be conducted through a more formal process, following a protocol that allows for deeper reflection with colleagues. In this approach, you will need another colleague, or even a group of colleagues, to participate. Selkrig and Keamy (2015) adapted a tuning protocol for pre-service teachers in Victoria to enable them to map their own progress against the Victoria Institute of Teaching's standards. I have further adapted this protocol (Figure 77) to be more specific to differentiation. You may want to use this protocol as a starting point when engaging in collegial conversations, adapting as you see necessary.

Figure 77: Adapted protocol for collegial conversations about differentiation

Presentation (4 mins)

The teacher makes a presentation on their differentiation efforts. They highlight student samples of work, teaching materials and resources, and the impact of their differentiation efforts on student growth and achievement.

Clarifying questions (2 mins)

Participants can ask clarifying questions to get pieces of information from the presentation that were perhaps omitted. Questions are asked to further understand the context of the presentation.

Pause for reflection (1 min)

Participants use this time to write down feedback they would like to share.

Warm feedback (3 mins)

Participants draw attention to the aspects of differentiation that they think are especially strong. Participants recognise the challenges the teacher may be experiencing in differentiation implementation. The aim of participants here is to help the presenter see value they might not have seen themselves in their presentation. Presenters take notes but do not respond.

Cool feedback (3 mins)

Participants pose questions to the presenter to make them wonder about differentiation, helping them to delve deeper into differentiation, outlining any confusion they might have. They share their concerns, issues or ideas that are worth exploring. Presenters do not respond yet.

Respond and open conversation (2 mins)

This is an opportunity for the presenter to respond to the questions and comments. Participants are quiet, allowing the presenter to speak.

Collegial conversations stand as a cornerstone for the ongoing growth and professional development of teachers. These discussions create lively spaces where educators exchange ideas, share experiences and explore diverse perspectives. They offer a platform to dissect teaching methodologies such as differentiation, analyse student engagement strategies, and collaborate on innovative approaches to pedagogy. Being a participant in a collegial conversation may allow you to learn more about how other teachers approach differentiation in their classrooms, giving you new ideas. Through these conversations, teachers gain fresh insights, refine their practices, and stay attuned to emerging trends in education. The camaraderie and collective wisdom fostered within collegial interactions not only enhance teaching effectiveness but also nurture a culture of lifelong learning among educators, ultimately benefiting both teachers and students alike.

Professional learning communities

Professional learning communities (PLCs) are groups of educators, typically from the same school or educational institution, who come together regularly to share expertise and work collaboratively to improve teaching skills and student learning outcomes (Hudson, 2023). I have facilitated PLCs across many of my workplaces, and one of the biggest reasons I love them is the sense of collegiality they foster. When I worked for the Department for Education in South Australia as a Curriculum Lead, we created PLCs that allowed teachers from across 30 schools to come together – teachers from a variety of schools, working together twice a term for a year – which was one of the most rewarding ways I saw teachers grow. According to the State Government of Victoria (2019), there are 10 principles of effective PLCs (Figure 78).

Figure 78: The 10 principles of effective PLCs
(State Government of Victoria, 2019)

1. **Student learning focus:** School improvement starts with an unwavering focus on student learning.
2. **Collective responsibility:** For every child to achieve, every adult must take responsibility for their learning.
3. **Instructional leadership:** Effective school leaders focus on teaching and learning.
4. **Collective efficacy:** Teachers make better instructional decisions together.

5. **Adult learning:** Teachers learn best with others, on the job.

6. **Privileged time:** Effective schools provide time and forums for teacher conversations about student learning.

7. **Continuous improvement:** Effective teams improve through recurring cycles of diagnosing student learning needs, and planning, implementing and evaluating teaching responses to them.

8. **Evidence-driven:** Effective professional learning and practice are evidence-based and data-driven.

9. **System focus:** The most effective school leaders contribute to the success of other schools.

10. **Integrated regional support:** Schools in improving systems are supported by teams of experts who know the communities they work in.

When thinking about a PLC for differentiation, you need to consider having a shared goal, such as increasing teacher knowledge, understanding and implementing differentiation, or increasing student motivation by targeting interests and learner preferences. This shared goal needs to be developed by you and your PLC. You and your PLC need to determine how often you will meet, and the goals you will need to accomplish before each meeting.

One of my most successful PLCs in differentiation was when we met twice a term, usually around week 3 and week 8. Our shared goal was to trial new differentiation strategies in the classroom and share with one another the challenges and successes we had. It was such a fantastic PLC, and as we grew more collegial with one another, we could really be honest about our progress. While we never measured it, there was a sense that we became more confident about differentiation the more times we met. We held each other accountable, ensuring that our goals were met before each session.

There are five key steps that you need to take in order to facilitate a PLC (Figure 79). It is important to remember that while you may see some similarities with learning walks, the creation of a PLC is a commitment between you and interested and willing colleagues, to learn new topics, share ideas and solve problems in a particular area. In this context, I will be highlighting the steps that can be taken to create a PLC that is linked to differentiation. Of course, you need to consider your and your PLC's individual experiences and knowledge – you may all have a good grasp of what differentiation is, and therefore may only focus on sharing strategies, while other PLCs focused on differentiation may be working towards creating policy and shared vision for differentiation across the school. What I offer here are some suggestions and starting points.

PLCs could incorporate time for teachers to share successes in differentiation implementation with one another, promoting collegial conversations. Collegial conversations could facilitate the development of greater self-efficacy, given that Bandura (1997) highlighted verbal and social persuasion as an effective way of increasing self-efficacy. Teachers could provide encouragement to one another in trialling new differentiation implementation strategies.

Figure 79: Five-step process for differentiation PLCs adapted from Wald and Castleberry (2000)

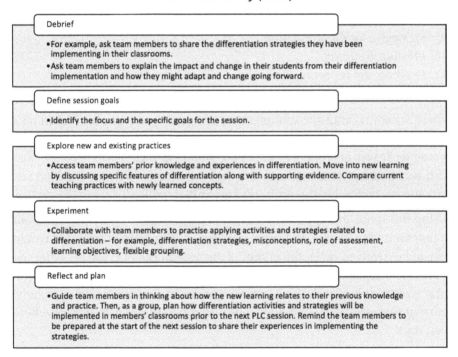

A good starting point, to determine what to focus on first, is to pre-assess teachers' existing knowledge, skills and understanding of differentiation. Have them detail what they believe differentiation is, as well as determining their confidence in implementing a range of differentiation strategies and techniques, such as the creation of KUD goals for learning objectives. You may even find this book beneficial for your PLC in guiding them through the steps of differentiation. Much like the topics in this book, PLC session topics could be, but are not limited to:

1. Defining what differentiation is (and is not!)
2. Exploring the connection between differentiation and inclusive education
3. Exploring current teaching practices
4. Exploring the mandated curriculum
5. Creation of learning objectives for what students should know, understand and be able to do
6. The role of assessment (pre-assessment, formative and summative) in differentiation
7. Differentiation of content, process and product
8. Differentiation according to readiness, interests and learner preferences
9. Strategies for differentiation
10. Flexible grouping
11. Grading and reporting in the differentiated classroom
12. School-wide differentiation.

There are some fantastic resources that can guide you and your PLC in how to undertake a PLC in your school. The Victorian Government does this particularly well and offers a range of resources and guides to help you. You can access many of these from this website: https://www2.education.vic. gov.au/pal/professional-learning-communities/policy.

Using the space in Supporting Activity 4 (page 165), start by planning out a potential PLC for you and some colleagues. Think about who you would like to be involved, what the potential purpose of the PLC will be, what the potential schedule could look like, and what topics it could focus on. You may want to consider drafting some questions to gauge potential members' current understanding and application of differentiation, to inform where you start.

Finally, schools need to create PLCs that support teachers in differentiating and maximising their time, given that they have been shown to be highly effective in upskilling teachers (Prenger et al., 2019). While it will cost schools money to allocate teachers time for professional development and to hire relief teachers, teachers will be able to upskill in differentiation and become more effective and capable in catering for student variance. If you are a school leader reading this, and want your staff to improve in their differentiation implementation and understanding, I encourage you to invest in PLCs. When teachers are more efficacious in differentiation, which PLCs promote, they are more likely to share their practices with colleagues, creating a ripple effect in upskilling teachers in differentiation. Be a catalyst for change in this area.

Teaching sprints

I am a huge fan of teaching sprints, a set of protocols that allow you to take a team-based approach to professional development, doing so in a focused and manageable way (Breakspear, 2020). Teaching sprints are relatively new in education, and while there has not been a considerable amount of research completed on their effectiveness, they do allow you to really narrow down a focus of professional development, work together with others, and be supported by one another, to achieve an end goal. They are, in essence, very similar to PLCs; however, teaching sprints have three phases (Breakspear, 2020): (1) prepare, (2) sprint and (3) review (see Figure 80 overleaf). In the prepare phase, you and your team work together to identify a focus for improvement – for example, creating quality learning objectives for what students should know, understand and be able to do. In this phase, you may consult research on how best to work towards the focus for improvement. The second phase, the sprint phase, is all about taking the theory and turning it into practice. Over a period of time, usually 2–4 weeks, team members "sprint" together, implementing new approaches and adapting as needed. This is where you would implement differentiation in your classroom, for example, all members sprinting for 2–4 weeks on ensuring they have KUD goals for each lesson. There are check-ins to ensure team members are supported. Lastly, the review phase is about reflection on the learning from the sprint phase, thinking about changes to teaching practice and the evidence of impact.

I would encourage you to look at Breakspear's website on teaching sprints, as he has various protocols that can help guide you in your teaching sprints, such as check-in protocols, review protocols and planners. An example of a potential teaching sprint is provided overleaf (Figure 81).

Figure 80: Three phases of teaching sprints

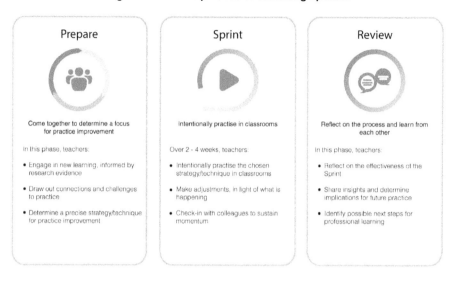

Prepare	Sprint	Review
Come together to determine a focus for practice improvement	Intentionally practise in classrooms	Reflect on the process and learn from each other
In this phase, teachers:	Over 2 - 4 weeks, teachers:	In this phase, teachers:
• Engage in new learning, informed by research evidence	• Intentionally practise the chosen strategy/technique in classrooms	• Reflect on the effectiveness of the Sprint
• Draw out connections and challenges to practice	• Make adjustments, in light of what is happening	• Share insights and determine implications for future practice
• Determine a precise strategy/technique for practice improvement	• Check-in with colleagues to sustain momentum	• Identify possible next steps for professional learning

SOURCE: BREAKSPEAR (2020).

Figure 81: Example of possible teaching sprint

Prepare
Team created.
Team engage in differentiation readings, such as books and journal articles.
Team decide on specific differentiation practice they would like to improve on. For example, using flexible grouping.

Sprint
Teachers intentionally practise use of flexible grouping throughout 4 weeks.
Teachers check in with each other twice within the month, making adjustments or supporting others to implement flexible grouping.

Review
Team come together to reflect on the sprint and share insights on how well they implemented flexible grouping, as well as challenges faced.
Team identify next steps for professional learning, such as another sprint.

What I love most about teaching sprints is their supportive nature. You do not sprint alone, nor are you left to your own devices as you are sprinting – you are supported through the journey. We know that when teachers try new teaching strategies and succeed in them, they are more likely to continue using them. In the case of differentiation, if teachers have challenges or fail with a particular differentiation strategy, they are quick to give up (Porta, 2023); hence, support is crucial to ongoing change and building of self-efficacy. Moreover, in my research, it was evident that many of the teachers

I interviewed were effective in differentiation practices that were familiar to them, but failure to branch out beyond their comfort zone meant that teachers were employing only familiar differentiation strategies in their lessons (Porta, 2023). This is where teaching sprints are valuable, in that they help teachers to move out of their comfort zone in supported ways. Use the template in Supporting Activity 5 (page 166) to plan out a first potential teaching sprint in differentiation.

Chapter summary and reflection

This chapter has provided you with the basis for reflecting on your attitudes and self-efficacy in differentiation. You have explored a variety of modes of professional development that can support you and your colleagues in your differentiation journey and contribute to high-quality professional development. Many practical starting points have been presented to you, encouraging you to work collaboratively with your colleagues, to become more confident and skilled in differentiation. Using the reflection template below, reflect on the learning you have gained from this chapter.

What did you find most relevant?

_____

_____

What was the most impactful and emotional learning?

_____

_____

What did you find most interesting?

_____

_____

What do you want to know more about?

_____

_____

Supporting Activity 1

Acknowledge your attitude towards inclusion and differentiation

Affective	
Behaviour	
Cognitive	

Supporting Activity 2

Self-efficacy experiences

Mastery experiences	
Vicarious experiences	
Social persuasion	
Psychological feedback	

Supporting Activity 3

Reflection on what you feel you need to improve in relation to your attitude and self-efficacy in differentiation.

Supporting Activity 4

Potential plan for differentiation PLC

Supporting Activity 5

Template for teaching sprint plan

Prepare	Sprint	Review

CHAPTER 8

Dance partners

"Dance every performance as if it were your last."

- ERIK BRUHN

Learning objectives

By the end of this chapter:

- Teachers will understand that differentiation is a journey that encompasses continuous growth and reflection, and requires leadership support.
- Teachers will know that leadership support is crucial for building an effective culture of differentiation, with leaders serving as enablers in differentiation practices.
- Teachers will be able to develop policy and reflect on their school leadership to find ways to promote whole school differentiation.

Before you begin this chapter, I want you to look at the following scenario (Figure 82). Perhaps this scenario is familiar to you as a school leader, or perhaps you have been subjected to random and unrelated professional development sessions during your schooling year as a teacher. These one-off sessions, while informative, do not in my opinion lead to sustainable change in teaching practices, teacher attitudes and self-efficacy. While I am not saying that the one-off professional development session is not valuable (as I have certainly learned many new things from these one-offs), I see teachers leave these sessions and perhaps try something new that week but forget about it soon after. Hence, change is not sustained. I showed Figure 82 to a room full of teachers, leaders and education professionals during a conference and they all giggled as I discussed the scenario – perhaps because it resonated with many of them. And yet, the one-off professional development session is still very common! I argue that a narrow and deep focus for professional development, and indeed, for differentiation learning and upskilling, is more effective.

In the previous chapter, we explored the various modalities for professional development, to enhance your understanding and skills in differentiation. In this chapter, we explore the role of school leadership teams in becoming enablers to help you and your colleagues to differentiate effectively in your classrooms. The aim here is to explore how leaders can help to build a sustainable culture of differentiation. We will journey through the role of policy in differentiation, as a means to help teachers and staff better understand what differentiation is and is not, while guiding teachers in their differentiation practice. Hence, school leadership teams may be seen as your dance partners in differentiation implementation.

Figure 82: Scenario of school leadership meeting

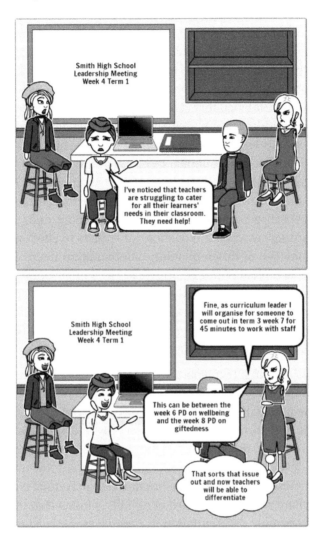

School leaders play a crucial role in ensuring that you and your colleagues can differentiate effectively in your classrooms. You may already be a leader in a school, or work with other leaders, in which case this chapter presents ways you can help facilitate your teachers in differentiation. Leaders significantly impact upon teachers' use of differentiation (Goddard et al., 2019) and leaders need to commit to upskilling teachers in differentiation over a sustained period of time, rather than through one-off professional development sessions (Porta, 2023; Sharp et al., 2018). Commitment is the operative word here. For teachers to be effective differentiators, leaders must commit to differentiation for a period of time.

Educational or school leaders are those who hold coordination, assistant principal, deputy principal and principal roles. Research on how educational leaders have engaged in the philosophy, culture and practices of differentiation in schools is minimal (Jarvis et al., 2016). However, there is emerging evidence that school leaders have an impact on student achievement (Goddard et al., 2019). More specifically, instructional leadership – where leaders place teaching and learning at the forefront of school decision making – appears to be a positive predictor of student success (Gumus et al., 2018). Hallinger (2005) suggests that instructional leadership is made up of three key dimensions: (1) defining the school's goals, (2) managing the instructional program and curriculum, and (3) promoting a positive learning environment. Hence, for leaders to effectively embed a culture and practice of differentiation, differentiation needs to form part of their strategic direction and be prioritised as a philosophy teachers can use for instruction. Schools have varying degrees of and organisational structures for leadership worldwide, and the way a school is organised impacts upon the school's vision and learning experiences (Organisation for Economic Cooperation and Development, 2016).

School leaders play an integral part in the way schools are managed and the direction schools take with professional development. School leadership teams have been seen to influence the professional development programs in which their staff participate. In a study at only one Australian secondary school, Sharp et al. (2018) emphasised the need for sustained and contextual professional development in differentiation, to support the embedment of a culture of inclusive education. In a broader research study encompassing 95 US elementary schools, Goddard et al. (2019) found that teachers were more likely to employ differentiation in their classrooms when supported by strong leadership. These researchers also found that when leaders supported teachers, teachers reportedly differentiated more in their school. In Serbia, Ninkovi et al. (2022) investigated the effect of transformational leadership on teachers' use of differentiation. They found that when transformational leadership – where leaders work with their teams to create change – was present, teachers participated more in cooperative activities, leading to more frequent differentiation implementation. Thus, leadership support in differentiation may directly or indirectly influence the provision of differentiation in school classrooms. This international research highlights that leadership teams play a key role in encouraging teachers to differentiate.

Committing to differentiation does not just happen overnight – depending on your role, you need to have your school leadership team understand the *why* and the impact that differentiation will have on students, to gain buy-in by this team. This may mean that you have to work with the school leaders in the first instance, before introducing differentiation professional development structures to the wider teaching and support staff.

Gibbs and McKay (2021) conducted a systematic literature review on differentiation practices in Australian mainstream classrooms and reviewed six Australian studies. They found that ongoing professional learning, as well as coaching on differentiation, is necessary for effective differentiation implementation; however, these practices must also be supported by leaders. One of the studies reviewed was Jarvis et al. (2016), which reported the views of eight leaders. Jarvis and her colleagues found that there was a need for leaders to develop a shared vision of differentiation and to become enablers for differentiation. Hence, developing a shared vision of what differentiation should look like at your site, and how you will achieve this vision, could be an effective starting point.

School leaders as dance partners for differentiation improvement

If you want to waltz, you will first need to find a dance partner. Similarly, school leaders are the partners you will need in your dance of differentiation – enabling you (and your colleagues) to improve upon your practice. We know from research (Jarvis et al., 2016; Porta et al., 2024) that school leaders have an impact on how teachers understand and implement differentiation. While I have detailed in the previous chapter many ways that professional development can occur to improve teachers' differentiation practices, school leaders and administrators need to be prepared to facilitate these modes of professional development, as well as providing teachers with the time to do so. Upskilling, coaching and professional development also require a financial commitment that schools will need to weigh up before committing. Using staff who differentiate well to highlight their practices to the wider school staff influences others to do the same – the ripple effect! In contrast, if differentiation is not being practised well by teaching staff, bringing in experts to get the ball rolling can be just as effective. A whole-school approach will be more effective in creating change in both teacher attitudes and self-efficacy, not just in differentiation but in inclusive education too. Hence, when planning out the year, remember that the learning walks you and your teams will take, the teaching sprints you and your colleagues will engage in, the range of PLCs that will be created on various aspects of differentiation, and the promotion of collegial conversations will all be beneficial.

Given the time-poor nature of teaching, however, giving teachers more time may not be feasible for many schools; as such, promoting differentiation through collaborative discussions with colleagues in and beyond one's faculty may be more meaningful, realistic and practical if this form of engagement is sustained rather than being a sporadic focus of the school. When made authentic – that is to say, practical and relevant to teachers – professional development can increase teachers' knowledge and skills (Kousa & Aksela, 2019). Thus, school leaders are encouraged to make decisions that allow for differentiation upskilling that suits their schooling context.

If you are a school leader, I encourage you to critically evaluate your attitude towards differentiation, and inclusion too, if you have not engaged in Chapter 7 of this book. A school I worked at for a number of years did not have a leadership team who valued differentiation or inclusive education. They said they did, but in reality they had an integration model that they were happy with and saw no reason to change. They wanted teachers to differentiate, but not to the extent where they would allow teachers time for professional development in differentiation. Therefore, since the value placed on such upskilling was minimal, there was never going to be a great impact on differentiation. This is not about looking back and judging the school for not valuing inclusive education. In fact, the lack of value placed on inclusive education told me that perhaps the leadership team did not fully understand what inclusive education is and how it translates to classroom practices and school structures and processes. To implement the professional development modes discussed in the previous chapter, a commitment of time, resources and money is needed, to avoid running the risk of superficial understanding and application of differentiation in classrooms. You also run the risk of having differentiation being seen as an *add-on* and just another professional development topic. This is detrimental.

I believe that, in order for teachers to start differentiating well, you cannot just jump into teaching them about the various differentiation strategies. You know from Chapter 1 that differentiation is not just a set of strategies but is a philosophy and set of principles, and understanding these before learning the strategies sets the foundation for differentiation implementation. From my research, and after reviewing much of the research on differentiation across Australia and the world, I developed a framework to assist schools in understanding the aspects they need to apply, to allow differentiation to become sustainable, and not just a one-off. This framework is depicted in Figure 83, and I will outline each of the components later in this chapter.

Figure 83: Building a sustainable culture of differentiation

Getting on the same page
Establishing a collective understanding
and responsibility for differentiation

**Allaying differentiation
misconceptions**
Differentiation is established in general teaching
and learning policies

**Practical professional
development**
Setting up sustained PD opportunities with practical
focus (PLCs, learning, walks/talks, teaching sprints)

**Establishing support
mechanisms**
Creating a buddy system, encouraging
collegial conversations, sharing good practice

**Moving beyond
one's comfort zone**
Encouraging teachers to trial
new differentiation strategies

**Differentiation
readiness**
Moving beyond student
labels and diagnoses

Student agency
Co-constructing
differentiation lessons
with students

Getting on the same page and allaying differentiation misconceptions

When I started working with schools to help them with differentiation implementation, my aim was to get all staff on the same page, which I often termed *getting your ducks in a row*. In this section of the framework, it was important to help all staff, including leadership teams, to develop a collective understanding of and responsibility for differentiation. One of the schools I worked with (which I won't identify here) wanted all of its staff to be good differentiators and to embrace differentiation. While this was a noble goal for the school, I found that the school's leadership team were not passionate about inclusive education, wanting students with additional needs to be outside of the mainstream classroom. As the leadership team did not value inclusion, this meant that staff often questioned why they should use more inclusive practices if the leadership team themselves did not value it. It was a valid point. While my aim here is not to say that the school was doing a poor job, because they actually excelled in many areas of professional development, the leadership team's resistance to inclusive education meant that others, such as teaching staff, did not see as much value in it as they might have, should they have had a supportive leadership team.

This drove me to get staff on the same page, so we could upskill together and support one another. This involved creating policies, procedures and guidelines on inclusive education and differentiation. For example, we created guidelines on how school support staff could be utilised within the mainstream classroom, and how they could support the differentiation decisions of teachers. It also meant we needed to review our current practices regarding inclusive education, looking at areas that needed to change. It was an uncomfortable time. It required challenging staff's thinking about inclusion, as well as outlining and extending our vision to the wider community. We dispelled the myths and misconceptions of differentiation and inclusion, as I have done earlier in this book, to ensure a common understanding. I worked with the school to develop their collective responsibility, establishing that no one, no matter their position, is exempt from creating a differentiated classroom, and that we all need to work towards inclusive education. You need to become attuned to teachers' perceptions of differentiation and inclusive education to be better informed and make more informed decisions about where to go. Similarly, we involved many community members and kept parents informed, so they too could develop a deeper understanding of what inclusive education meant for the school.

I found that teachers had a limited understanding of what differentiation is and whom it is for. Similarly, they had a limited understanding of what inclusion and inclusive education are too. While not a policy, my team and I took the approach of trying to shape the staff's understanding of inclusive education first, then helping them to understand how differentiation fits into the picture of inclusive education. I wanted to ensure our school community understood this too. So, we started by developing a statement for inclusive education, outlining the principles we wanted to uphold in our school. These principles are outlined in Figure 84 and based on the principles of inclusion by Ainscow (2009). This was our starting point, where we started to design a policy that promoted inclusive education and the importance of differentiation for all.

Figure 84: Principles of inclusive education

Presence

All students are present in the classroom, not just physically, but they are provided with the necessary supports and guidance to access the curriculum and classroom activities.

Participation

All students are actively supported to participate in a respectful and meaningful way in all classroom activities.

Progress

All students have the right to learn and make reasonable progress in their learning, regardless of their starting point, education needs, or level of understanding.

Belonging

All teachers must help students develop a sense of belonging and social and emotional connection to the classroom environment.

SOURCE: ADAPTED FROM AINSCOW (2009).

We started to align policy with leadership and leadership with policy, planning how we would assist teachers in understanding the policy and leadership in understanding their role as enablers for teachers and other relevant staff. Some of what we will explore below will link with the previous chapter, regarding professional development. After all, leadership teams decide the focus for professional development in schools, including how to approach differentiation professional development.

There is limited research on differentiation and curriculum policies in Australia (Eikeland & Ohna, 2022; Frankling et al., 2017); however, when policies do exist, there is an increased awareness of differentiation and a change in teachers' understanding and expectations (Sharp et al., 2018). Furthermore, school policies may also create standards of quality for teaching and learning (Allen et al., 2021) – thus, creating a policy for differentiation may improve teacher quality in its use. It is for these reasons that you may want to look at the policies or guidance documents of your school, to see if they are, or could be, used to encourage teachers to utilise differentiation in their classrooms. You may even go broader, looking at creating a policy that encompasses how teachers and school community members intend to achieve inclusive education at your school site. This was what I did with one of the schools I worked with, and from my professional observations, teachers began to embrace inclusive education more.

During my research (Porta et al., 2024), it was not quite clear as to whether policies linked to differentiation had an impact on the way teachers implemented differentiation. Some of the teachers I interviewed did not care much about policies, differentiating in the way they knew best. There was, however, a surprising finding: all of my participants, bar one, held the misconception that differentiation was a special education practice, exclusively for students with learning difficulties and/or disabilities. They did not view differentiation as a practice for all students, as differentiation is intended to be. These same teachers spoke about differentiation being in special education policies; hence, their view on who differentiation is for may have been shaped by differentiation being in special education policies. Only one participant recognised that differentiation is for all students, and she was a deputy principal at the time. She knew the importance of differentiation being for all, and she wrote about the importance of differentiation in her school's general teaching and learning policy. Interestingly, other teachers in the same school were not aware of this.

According to Graham (2023), education policy prescribes what needs to happen to solve a problem. Hence, outlining the importance of differentiation in the classroom, and how it can be implemented, while addressing and dispelling differentiation misconceptions, may help teachers implement differentiation well. Graham (2023) further argues that when there are shared opportunities to build knowledge and skills, and a network of support, this can drive change, moving from policy intent to policy implementation. Having a policy on differentiation implementation will not in itself be enough to drive change, which is why other elements of sustained professional development are required. It is important that differentiation not be seen as a teaching practice and philosophy only for students with learning difficulties, disabilities and/or special needs. Rather, it is a tier 1 process within the multitiered systems of support that can be provided to all students.

Using the space in Supporting Activity 1 or the "School policy treasure hunt" (page 184), find out if there are any policies in your school that support teachers in implementing differentiation. Outline where this is found – perhaps it is part of a special education or inclusive education policy? Or it may not be in any policy at all. Reflect on how differentiation can be embedded into your school's policies to ensure it is conveyed more accurately to school teachers, staff and the wider community. Make a plan to discuss this with your leadership team. Think about what should be included in order to *get your ducks in a row*.

A clear policy declaring that differentiation is for all students and not just for those with disabilities or other complex needs may encourage all teachers – and not just those who teach students with additional needs – to feel responsible for implementing differentiation. Including differentiation in general teaching and learning policies prevents differentiation being conceptualised as a philosophy restricted to special education students.

Practical professional development and establishing support mechanisms

Once you have established a collective understanding and responsibility for differentiation, and dispelled any misconceptions regarding differentiation and inclusive education, you are ready to start to implement relevant and sustained professional development methods into your school. You may have already been implementing some professional development to help get leadership and teachers on the same page; however, the aim now is to implement professional development that is sustained and supportive.

I know many of you reading this will have been subjected to the termly professional development session – usually the day before students come back to school and usually on completely different topics from one another with no connection between them. Do not get me wrong, I have certainly been to valuable professional development sessions on the professional development days; however, they are rarely followed up with any actions. By that I mean: we sit, we listen and then we return to our classes, having never really implemented or trialled anything we learned. There is often a lack of connection to curriculum and students, and this has been well-established in the research (Yoon et al., 2007). Practical experience and ongoing and sustained professional development in differentiation are vital to ensure that teachers can go beyond what they are familiar with and develop a deeper understanding of differentiation strategies and the philosophy as a whole. Similarly, professional development needs to focus on differentiating for all learners and the diversity that exists in the classroom to ensure that differentiation implementation is understood as a framework and philosophy for all students (Porta, 2023). You will need to explore some of the ways that you can create ongoing professional development, beyond just the termly professional development.

Before you move on, use the space in Supporting Activity 2 (page 184) to reflect on your own professional development experiences – *What went well? What could be done better to drive change in your teaching practice?* Think about what you would like to see in a professional development program to help you grow as a teacher.

Comfort zone, readiness and student voice

The last three elements of the framework for building a sustainable culture of differentiation are: moving teachers beyond their comfort zone, addressing readiness, and utilising the student voice in the differentiated classroom. Much of my research found that teachers had various differentiation strategies in their pedagogy that they were familiar and comfortable with (Porta, 2023). This is a fantastic strength! Each of the teachers I interviewed utilised different differentiation strategies but tended to stick in their comfort zone. There are two things here that you should try to achieve. First, teachers who are utilising differentiation strategies well, and confidently, should have the opportunity to share this with other colleagues. Why? Because colleagues will be able to learn from one another. When I taught Year 10 Psychology, I set myself a goal of utilising a range of flexible grouping strategies, and I invited all staff across the school to visit my classroom – including teacher aides. In the beginning, two people floated in and out of my lessons; however, over the four weeks, the number of teachers that visited increased. I had teachers visiting my office to ask for advice or discuss how they could adapt flexible grouping to suit their classroom context. While I may not have influenced the entire school, this simple practice of sharing allowed a few teachers to trial a new strategy. Second, you should encourage colleagues who are in their comfort zone with differentiation strategies to branch out and expand their repertoire as a means of growing in their differentiation journey. To achieve this, I ran a series of weekly professional development sessions for a term, inviting staff to attend and participate. The idea behind these practical development sessions was that teachers would be actively designing differentiated learning experiences throughout the workshops. While attendance numbers were small – likely due to my after-school time slot – I had a consistent turnout of approximately five teachers. One of the teachers had never created a tiered lesson before, as she had taught in China for most of her career, where she said that tiered lessons were not really a thing. She expressed to me that she felt that differentiation was not her strong point, but she had a willingness to learn. She astounded me with her positive attitude, creating a series of tiered lessons over the course of the term, and implementing these with her students. I remember her telling me how scared she was to try tiering, but how happy she felt after giving it a go. It was beautiful to watch the impact that these sessions had on the teachers who participated.

As I have discussed earlier, many teachers assume that differentiation is exclusively for students with learning difficulties, disabilities and/or other special needs. As teachers become educated and upskilled in differentiation, they start to differentiate (if they aren't already) by readiness. When I conducted my PhD research (Porta, 2023), many teachers were differentiating according to student labels or diagnoses. For example, they were assuming that students with learning difficulties were always of lower readiness, or that all students who were on the autism spectrum required scaffolds. While I am certainly not arguing that these diagnoses are not necessary, relying solely upon them for differentiation runs the risk of boxing students in. You cannot just assume that the students with learning difficulties or other identified learning needs will always be in the lower readiness group. Hence, educating teachers on the importance of ongoing assessment and using this assessment in differentiation decisions is crucial.

The teachers I interviewed in my PhD research had varying levels of self-efficacy in differentiation, but there was one teacher who was a particular standout. She stated that she was confident in differentiating and had extensive knowledge and understanding of what differentiation was and was not. She also said that she was consistent in her application of differentiation – so much so that she began to incorporate student agency and voice in the planning of her differentiation. For example, she would co-construct her learning objectives with her students, prior to the lesson, having them provide input into what they would like to see throughout the lesson. She relinquished control of the lesson, giving students more choice. As you start to become more confident and efficacious in differentiation, you can start to involve students. In fact, research says that students want to have more voice and choice in their learning (Scarparolo & MacKinnon, 2022). The benefit of including student voice is that this will contribute to inclusive education outcomes for students. A word of caution here, and this is why student agency is the last layer of the onion in Figure 83 ("Building a sustainable culture of differentiation"): do not ask or expect teachers to include student agency and voice, such as lesson co-construction in differentiation, until they are confident and efficacious in differentiation. Allowing student choice and agency in their learning may be difficult for teachers who lack self-efficacy in differentiation implementation, or do not fully understand the philosophy of differentiation. Hence, trying to embed student agency early on in one's differentiation learning journey may contribute to feelings of being overwhelmed – leading to negative attitudes towards differentiation. Therefore, schools may need to make a commitment to upskilling teachers in practical differentiation implementation, rather than focusing on the theory of differentiation alone, and to supporting teachers in becoming confident in differentiation, before they begin to include student voice and agency in their classrooms. Similarly, teachers need to be taught how to develop strong relationships with students for differentiation implementation to become more effective.

Using the space in Supporting Activity 3 (page 184), reflect on your use of student agency and voice in your lessons. How have you utilised these before? How could you start incorporating student agency and voice in your lessons going forwards? In my experience, co-constructing differentiated lessons with students has been beneficial in strengthening my relationships with students, but again, it takes time. I would often spend the last few minutes of a lesson outlining potential foci for the next lesson. Here, I would ask students what they would like to focus on from a selection of potential topics/areas of study. Then I would guide them towards our KUDs, allowing them to further voice what activities or groupings they might like to see in the next lesson. At first, I found this co-construction awkward. I had to let go of the fact that I was relinquishing control of the class and that this was a good thing. I certainly did not co-construct every one of my lessons – but in one way or another, the majority of my lessons had some form of student voice or choice embedded into them. Persevere with the initial uncomfortableness and lean into the discomfort. This will subside the more you practise.

Where to from here?

There are many layers to building a sustainable culture of differentiation in a school, and it takes a serious commitment by school leaders to become enablers in this process. This is not easy. Schools have many competing demands and priorities, and differentiation is just one part of a bigger dance that's taking place. Not all schools will prioritise differentiation, or even inclusive education – mainly because of existing school structures, such as those favouring integration, and lack of expertise. You may be a school leader yourself who wants to take your school on an extensive and rigorous differentiation journey. I say to you: keep fighting and challenging leadership and teachers' perceptions and application of differentiation. Remember that differentiation forms part of inclusive education and – as established in Chapter 1 – inclusive education, like differentiation, is not just a teaching practice, but requires significant reform.

Think back to the scenario in Figure 82, highlighting an attitude that many school leadership teams have. Figure 85 depicts a revised version that would better serve teachers and your students. You may not be a leader in a school, but recognise the importance of differentiation. You can, much like I did, influence other teachers and staff within your own sphere of influence. Share your classroom practices with others, talk with others about their successes and failures, and support one another to try new things.

Figure 85: Revised scenario of school leadership meeting

Conclusion and reflection

Well, what a journey we have been on – perhaps you feel like you have learned to tango, salsa and rhumba all in the one book! This book highlights some of the ways you can differentiate in your classrooms to achieve inclusive education and should serve as a reference point as you start your differentiation journey. Remember that confidence comes from trial and error, and recognise that when differentiation does not work for you, you should not give up on it, but make it work for you. Dancing takes a toll on the body, and requires energy. Therefore, it is not something you can do for hours on end. Differentiation also requires energy, meaning that you need to practise before you can undertake a sustained dance.

As you have reached the end of the final chapter of this book, I want you to reflect on your overall journey, and where you intend to go next. Perhaps this text has been a springboard for you, propelling you to start your differentiation journey. Or perhaps this text has been the focal point for a professional learning community for a period of time. Regardless, think about what is next for you and decide upon two clear goals for the term, semester or year that you can work towards.

Reflection on your differentiation journey thus far:

_____

_____

_____

_____

_____

Creation of two goals to work towards:

1. _____

2. _____

Supporting Activity 1

School policy treasure hunt

Supporting Activity 2

Reflection on past professional development

Supporting Activity 3

Incorporating student agency and voice

Conclusion

I love differentiation, and while I may be biased, I firmly believe that differentiation can allow you to develop as a teacher, in becoming more inclusive in your classrooms. I have seen the impact that differentiation can have on creating inclusive and equitable classrooms, and I want all students to be a part of an inclusive classroom.

It is my hope that reading this book has spurred you on to take the next step in your differentiation journey. Perhaps you are taking your first steps, starting by getting to know the curriculum really well, or perhaps you are ready to help others in your school to develop their self-efficacy in differentiation. No matter where you are at, I hope you have acquired some new knowledge.

Differentiation, like an intricate dance, embodies the rhythm of teaching – an art form where every step, every move, holds the promise of inclusivity and growth. As educators, our embrace of differentiation is not merely a choreographed routine; it is an invitation to sway with the melodies of diverse learning needs, creating a harmonious symphony within our classrooms.

In this intricate dance of pedagogy, complexity is our partner. It challenges us to refine our steps, experiment with new movements, and synchronise our efforts as a team. Trialling new strategies and harmonising our collective expertise are the key notes in this captivating melody of differentiation.

Purposefulness becomes our guiding tempo – a constant inquiry into the "why?" behind every differentiation strategy. It is the elegant pause between intention and actions, ensuring that every step we take is not just deliberate, but resonates deeply with our students' needs and educational objectives.

Yet, this dance is not a solo performance. It is a collaborative ballet where educators join hands, sharing their experiences, learning from each other's rhythms and co-creating an inclusive educational ensemble. Inclusive education, much like a vibrant dance, requires synchronised movements from every member of our educational troupe.

While we have made strides towards inclusive education in Australia, our journey is not over. Effective differentiation serves as a pivotal dance move – a graceful pivot contributing to the larger choreography of inclusivity in education. However, we know that true inclusive education comes about through, not just the teaching practices you employ in your classroom, but cultural and policy changes that put students at the centre of education. Be bold enough to push these boundaries as you dance.

So, let us continue to dance this beautiful, complex rhythm of differentiation. Embrace its intricacies, find joy in its challenges, and let it lead us towards a more inclusive education – a dance where every step shapes a brighter future for our learners.

Dance away, you amazing teacher!

References

Abawi, L., Fanshawe, M., Gilbey, K., Andersen, C., & Rogers, C. (2019). Celebrating diversity: focus on inclusion. In S. Carter (Ed.), *Opening eyes onto inclusion and diversity* (pp. 41–91). University of Southern Queensland.

Ainscow, M. (2009). Developing inclusive education systems: How can we move policies forward? In C. Giné (Ed.), *La educación inclusiva: De la exclusión a la plena participación de todo el alumnado*, (pp. 161–70). ICE/Horsori.

Allen, A. S., & Topolka-Jorissen, K. (2014). Using teacher learning walks to build capacity in a rural elementary school: Repurposing a supervisory tool. *Professional Development in Education, 40*(5), 822–37. https://doi.org/10.1080/19415257.2013.851104

Allen, K.-A., Reupert, A., & Oades, L. (2021). *Building better schools with evidence-based policy: Adaptable policy for teachers and school leaders.* Taylor & Francis.

American Academy. (n.d.). Multi-tiered system of supports (MTSS). https://www.aak8.org/apps/pages/aa-sss-rti

Arnup, J., & Bowles, T. (2016). Should I stay or should I go? Resilience as a protective factor for teachers' intention to leave the teaching profession. *Australian Journal of Education, 60*(3), 229–44. https://doi.org/10.1177/0004944116667620

Australian Curriculum, Assessment and Reporting Authority. (2023a). *The Australian Curriculum Version 9.0.* https://v9.australiancurriculum.edu.au/

Australian Curriculum, Assessment and Reporting Authority. (2023b). *General capabilities.* https://v9.australiancurriculum.edu.au/f-10-curriculum/f-10-curriculum-overview/general-capabilities

Australian Curriculum, Assessment and Reporting Authority. (2023c). *Implications for teaching, assessing and reporting.* https://www.australiancurriculum.edu.au/f-10-curriculum/implications-for-teaching-assessing-and-reporting/

Australian Curriculum, Assessment and Reporting Authority. (2023d). *Student diversity.* https://v9.australiancurriculum.edu.au/student-diversity

Australian Government. (2023a). *National Teacher Workforce Action Plan.* https://www.education.gov.au/national-teacher-workforce-action-plan

Australian Government. (2023b). *Strong beginnings: Report of the Teacher Education Expert Panel.* Retrieved from https://www.education.gov.au/quality-initial-teacher-education-review/resources/strong-beginnings-report-teacher-education-expert-panel

Australian Institute for Teaching and School Leadership [AITSL]. (2017). *Australian professional standards for teachers.* https://www.aitsl.edu.au/standards

Bambara, L. M., Janney, R., & Snell, M. E. (2015). *Behavior support.* Brookes Publishing.

Bandura, A. (1997). *Self-efficacy: the exercise of control.* W. H. Freeman.

Banks, J. (2022). Multi-tiered systems of support: A roadmap for achieving an inclusive education system. In *The inclusion dialogue* (pp. 36–53). Taylor & Francis Group. https://doi.org/10.4324/9781003263425-4

Barker, K., Poed, S., & Whitefield, P. (2022). *School-wide positive behaviour support: The Australian handbook*. Taylor & Francis Group.

Barrett, T. (2023). *Uplevel your prompt craft in ChatGPT with the CREATE framework*. https://edte.ch/blog/2023/01/22/create-framework/?v=3a1ed7090bfa

Berman, J., Graham, L., Bellert, A., & McKay-Brown, L. (2023). *Responsive teaching for sustainable learning: A framework for inclusive education*. Taylor & Francis.

Booth, T., & Ainscow, M. (2002). *Index for inclusion: developing learning and participation in schools*. CSIE.

Börnert-Ringleb, M., Westphal, A., Zaruba, N., Gutmann, F., & Vock, M. (2020). The relationship between attitudes toward inclusion, beliefs about teaching and learning, and subsequent automatic evaluations amongst student teachers. *Frontiers in Education (Lausanne), 5*(1). https://doi.org/10.3389/feduc.2020.584464

Breakspear, S. (2020). *The teaching sprints process*. https://teachingsprints.com/process

CAST. (2023). *What is co-teaching? An introduction to co-teaching and inclusion*. https://publishing.cast.org/stories-resources/stories/co-teaching-introduction-inclusion-stein

Cawte, K. (2020). Teacher crisis: Critical events in the mid-career stage. *Australian Journal of Teacher Education, 45*(8), 75–92. https://doi.org/10.14221/ajte.2020v45n8.5

Children's Literacy Initiative. (n.d.). What is data driven instruction? https://cli.org/2015/04/02/what-is-data-driven-instruction/

Cologon, K. (2022). Is inclusive education really for everyone? Family stories of children and young people labelled with 'severe and multiple' or 'profound' 'disabilities'. *Research Papers in Education, 37*(3), 395–417. https://doi.org/10.1080/02671522.2020.1849372

Crispin, G. (2013) Our Education System. https://gayecrispin.wordpress.com/2013/03/17/our-education-system-poster/

Dack, H. (2019). Understanding teacher candidate misconceptions and concerns about differentiated instruction. *Teacher Educator, 54*(1), 22–45. https://doi.org/10.1080/08878730.2018.1485802

Dixon, S. (2005). Inclusion – Not segregation or integration is where a student with special needs belongs. *The Journal of Educational Thought (JET)/Revue de La Pensée Éducative, 33*–53.

Doubet, K. J. (2022). *The flexibly grouped classroom: How to organize learning for equity and growth*. ASCD.

Dulfer, N. (2019). Differentiation in the International Baccalaureate Diploma Programme. *Journal of Research in International Education, 18*(2), 142–68. http://dx.doi.org/10.1177/1475240919865654

Eagly, A. H., & Chaiken, S. (1998). Attitude structure and function. In *The Handbook of Social Psychology* (4th ed., Vol. 1, pp. 269–322). McGraw-Hill.

Eikeland, I., & Ohna, S. E. (2022). Differentiation in education: A configurative review. *Nordic Journal of Studies in Educational Policy*, 1–14. https://doi.org/10.1080/20020317.2022.2039351

Fisher, D., & Frey, N. (2014). Using teacher learning walks to improve instruction. *Principal Leadership, 14*(5), 58–61.

Frankling, T., Jarvis, J. M., & Bell, M. (2017). Leading secondary teachers' understandings and practices of differentiation through professional learning. *Leading & Managing, 23*(2), 72–86.

Furze, L. (2023). *Practical strategies for ChatGPT in education*. https://leonfurze.com/2023/01/23/practical-strategies-for-chatgpt-in-education/

Future Learn. (n.d.). Vygotsky's concept of the "Zone of Proximal Development". https://www.futurelearn.com/info/courses/differentiating-for-learning-stem/0/steps/15505

Gheyssens, E., Coubergs, C., Griful-Freixenet, I., Engels, N., & Struyven, K. (2020). Differentiated instruction: The diversity of teachers' philosophy and praxis to adapt teaching to students' interests, readiness and learning profiles. *International Journal of Inclusive Education, 26*(14), 1383–1400. https://doi.org/10.1080/13603116.2020.1812739

Gibbs, K., & McKay, L. (2021). Differentiated teaching practices of Australian mainstream classroom teachers: A systematic review and thematic analysis. *International Journal of Educational Research, 109*, 101799. https://doi.org/10.1016/j.ijer.2021.101799

Goddard, Y. L., Goddard, R. D., Bailes, L. P., & Nichols, R. (2019). From school leadership to differentiated instruction: A pathway to student learning in schools. *Elementary School Journal, 120*(2), 197–219. https://doi.org/10.1086/705827

Graham, L. (Ed.). (2019). *Inclusive education for the 21st century*. Taylor & Francis Group.

Graham, L. J. (2023). *Inclusive education for the 21st century: Theory, policy and practice* (2nd ed.). Routledge. https://doi.org/10.4324/9781003350897

Gumus, S., Bellibas, M. S., Esen, M., & Gumus, E. (2018). A systematic review of studies on leadership models in educational research from 1980 to 2014. *Educational Management Administration & Leadership, 46*(1), 25–48. https://doi.org/10.1177/1741143216659296

Hallinger, P. (2005). Instructional leadership and the school principal: A passing fancy that refuses to fade away. *Leadership and Policy in Schools, 4*(3), 221–39. https://doi.org/10.1080/15700760500244793

Harlin, R., Sirota, E., & Bailey, L. (2009). Review of research: The impact of teachers' expectations on diverse learners' academic outcomes. *Childhood Education, 85*(4), 253–56. https://doi.org/10.1080/00094056.2009.10523092

Hattie, J. A. C. (2003). Formative and summative interpretations of assessment information. https://assessment.tki.org.nz/content/download/6076/61425/version/1/file/formative-and-summative-assessment-%282003%29.pdf

Heffernan, A., Bright, D., Kim, M., Longmuir, F., & Magyar, B. (2022). 'I cannot sustain the workload and the emotional toll': Reasons behind Australian teachers' intentions to leave the profession. *Australian Journal of Education, 66*(2), 196–209. https://doi.org/10.1177/00049441221086654

Heffernan, A., Longmuir, F., Bright, D., & Kim, M. (2019). Perceptions of teachers and teaching in Australia. Monash University. https://www.monash.edu/thank-your-teacher/docs/Perceptions-of-Teachers-and-Teaching-in-Australia-report-Nov-2019.pdf

Hehir, T., Grindal, T., Freeman, B., Lamoreau, R., Borquaye, Y., & Burke, S. (2016). *A summary of the evidence on inclusive education*. Instituto Alano. https://alana.org.br/wp-content/uploads/2016/12/A_Summary_of_the_evidence_on_inclusive_education.pdf

Heick, T. (2021). What is Bloom's taxonomy? A definition for teachers. https://www.teachthought.com/learning/what-is-blooms-taxonomy

Hudson, C. (2023). A conceptual framework for understanding effective professional learning community (PLC) operation in schools. *Journal of Education*. https://doi.org/10.1177/00220574231197364

James-Ward, C., Fisher, D., Frey, N., & Lapp, D. (2013). *Using data to focus instructional improvement*. ASCD.

Jarvis, J. (2015). Inclusive classrooms and differentiation. In N. Weatherby-Fell (Ed.), *Learning to teach in the secondary school* (pp. 151–71). Cambridge University Press.

Jarvis, J. M., Bell, M., & Sharp, K. (2016). Leadership for differentiation: An appreciative inquiry of how educational leadership shapes pedagogical change. *Leading & Managing, 22*(1), 75–91.

Kousa, P., & Aksela, M. (2019). The needs for successful chemistry teaching in diverse classes: Teachers' beliefs and practices. *LUMAT, 7*(1), 79–100. https://doi.org/10.31129/LUMAT.7.1.390

Mills, M., Monk, S., Keddie, A., Renshaw, P., Christie, P., Geelan, D., & Gowlett, C. (2014). Differentiated learning: From policy to classroom. *Oxford Review of Education, 40*(3), 331–48. https://doi.org/10.1080/03054985.2014.911725

Monteiro, E., Kuok, A. C. H., Correia, A. M., Forlin, C., & Teixeira, V. (2019). Perceived efficacy of teachers in Macao and their alacrity to engage with inclusive education. *International Journal of Inclusive Education, 23*(1), 93–108. https://doi.org/10.1080/13603116.2018.1514762

New South Wales Government. (2022). *Strategies for differentiation.* https://education.nsw.gov.au/teaching-and-learning/professional-learning/teacher-quality-and-accreditation/strong-start-great-teachers/refining-practice/differentiating-learning/strategies-for-differentiation

Ninković, S., Knežević-Florić, O., & Đorđić, D. (2022). Transformational leadership and teachers' use of differentiated instruction in Serbian schools: Investigating the mediating effects of teacher collaboration and self-efficacy. *Educational Studies,* 1–20. https://doi.org/10.1080/03055698.2022.2081787

Oh-Young, C., & Filler, J. (2015). A meta-analysis of the effects of placement on academic and social skill outcome measures of students with disabilities. *Research in Developmental Disabilities, 47*, 80–92.

Organisation for Economic Cooperation and Development [OECD]. (2016). *What makes a school a learning organisation? A guide for policy makers, school leaders and teachers.* https://www.oecd.org/education/school/school-learning-organisation.pdf

Porta, T. (2023). *Differentiated instruction for students with learning difficulties in senior-secondary Australian schools: An inquiry of teacher attitudes and self-efficacy.* University of Southern Queensland.

Porta, T., & Todd, N. (2022). Differentiated instruction within senior secondary curriculum frameworks: A small-scale study of teacher views from an independent South Australian school. *The Curriculum Journal, 33*(4), 570–86. https://doi.org/10.1002/curj.157

Porta, T., & Todd, N. (2023). The impact of labelling students with learning difficulties on teacher self-efficacy in differentiated instruction. *Journal of Research in Special Educational Needs.* https://doi.org/10.1111/1471-3802.12619

Porta, T., Todd, N., & Gaunt, L. (2024). Australian senior-secondary teachers' perceptions of leadership and policy for differentiated instruction. *British Educational Research Journal, 00*, 1–21. https://doi.org/10.1002/berj.3967

Prenger, R., Poortman, C. L., & Handelzalts, A. (2019). The effects of networked professional learning communities. *Journal of Teacher Education, 70*(5), 441–52. https://doi.org/10.1177/0022487117753574

Reis, S. M., & Renzulli, J. S. (2005). *Curriculum compacting: An easy start to differentiating for high-potential students.* Prufrock Press Inc.

Renzulli, J., & Reis, S. (1992). The complete guide to modifying the regular curriculum for high ability students. *Creative Learning Press.*

Richler, D. (2012). Systemic barriers to inclusion. In C. Boyle & K. Topping (Eds.), *What works in inclusion* (pp. 176–87). Open University Press.

Riener, C., & Willingham, D. (2010). The myth of learning styles. *Change: The Magazine of Higher Learning, 42*, 32–35. http://dx.doi.org/10.1080/00091383.2010.503139

Roberts, J. L., & Inman, T. F. (2023). *Strategies for differentiating instruction: Best practices for the classroom* (4th ed.). Routledge. https://doi.org/10.4324/9781003330561

San Martin, C., Ramirez, C., Calvo, R., Muñoz-Martínez, Y., & Sharma, U. (2021). Chilean teachers' attitudes towards inclusive education, intention, and self-efficacy to implement inclusive practices. *Sustainability, 13*(4), 2300. https://www.mdpi.com/2071-1050/13/4/2300

Sands, D. J., Kozleski, E. B., & French, N. K. (2000). *Inclusive education for the 21st century: A new introduction to special education*. Wadsworth/Thomson Learning.

Scarparolo, G., & MacKinnon, S. (2022). Student voice as part of differentiated instruction: Students' perspectives. *Educational Review*, 1–18. https://doi.org/10.1080/00131911.2022.2047617

Scarparolo, G., & Subban, P. (2023). Differentiation and differentiated instruction: A philosophy and pedagogical approach to inclusive teaching and responsive, effective instruction. Chapter 1 (Australia). In *Differentiated instruction around the world: A global inclusive insight: Exploring differentiated instructional practice in general school education* (pp. 21–34). Waxman.

Scruggs, T., Mastropieri, M., & McDuffie, K. (2007). Co-teaching in inclusive classrooms: A metasynthesis of qualitative research. *Exceptional Children, 73*, 392–416. https://doi.org/10.1177/001440290707300401

Selkrig, M., & Keamy, K. (2015). Promoting a willingness to wonder: Moving from congenial to collegial conversations that encourage deep and critical reflection for teacher educators. *Teachers and Teaching, 21*(4), 421–36. https://doi.org/10.1080/13540602.2014.969104

Sharp, K., Jarvis, J. M., & McMillan, J. M. (2018). Leadership for differentiated instruction: Teachers' engagement with on-site professional learning at an Australian secondary school. *International Journal of Inclusive Education, 24*(2), 1–20. https://doi.org/10.1080/13603116.2018.1492639

Sharratt, L. (2018). Leading with knowledge in communities of practice. *Australian Educational Leader, 40*(4), 12–16.

Sileo, J. (2011). Co-teaching: Getting to know your partner. *TEACHING Exceptional Children, 43*, 32–38. https://doi.org/10.1177/004005991104300503

State Government of Victoria. (2019). *Professional learning communities*. https://www.education.vic.gov.au/school/teachers/management/improvement/plc/Pages/default.aspx

Sun, Y., & Xiao, L. (2021). Research trends and hotspots of differentiated instruction over the past two decades (2000–2020): A bibliometric analysis. *Educational Studies*, 1–17. https://doi.org/10.1080/03055698.2021.1937945

Todd, N., Gaunt, L., & Porta, T. (2022). Terminology and provision for students with learning difficulties: An examination of Australian state government education department websites. *Australian Journal of Teacher Education, 47*(7). https://doi.org/10.14221/ajte.2022v47n7.2

Tomlinson, C. (2001). *How to differentiate instruction in mixed-ability classrooms*. Pearson Education.

Tomlinson, C., Coleman, M., Allan, S., Udall, A., & Landrum, M. (1996). Interface between gifted education and general education: Toward communication, cooperation and collaboration. *Gifted Child Quarterly, 40*, 165–71. https://doi.org/10.1177/001698629604000308

Tomlinson, C. A. (1997). Good teaching for one and all: Does gifted education have an instructional identity? *Journal for the Education of the Gifted, 20*(2), 155–74. https://doi.org/10.1177/016235329602000201

Tomlinson, C. A. (2005). Grading and differentiation: Paradox or good practice? *Theory into Practice, 44*(3), 262–69. https://doi.org/10.1207/s15430421tip4403_11

Tomlinson, C. A. (2014). *The differentiated classroom: Responding to the needs of all learners.* ASCD.

Tomlinson, C. A. (2022). *Everybody's classroom: Differentiating for the shared and unique needs of diverse students.* Teachers College Press.

Tomlinson, C. A., & Allan, S. D. (2000). *Leadership for differentiating schools and classrooms.* ASCD.

Tomlinson, C. A., & Borland, J. H. (2022). *Everybody's classroom: Differentiating for the shared and unique needs of diverse students.* Teachers College Press.

Tomlinson, C. A., & McTighe, J. (2006). *Integrating differentiated instruction & understanding by design: Connecting content and kids.* ASCD.

Tomlinson, C. A., & Moon, T. R. (2013). *Assessment and student success in a differentiated classroom.* Association for Supervision & Curriculum Development.

United Nations. (2016). *General comment No. 4, Article 24: Right to inclusive education.* https://www.ohchr.org/Documents/HRBodies/CRPD/GC/RighttoEducation/CRPD-C-GC-4.doc

Vygotsky, L. S. (1978). *Mind in society: Development of higher psychological processes.* Harvard University Press. https://doi.org/10.2307/j.ctvjf9vz4

Vygotsky, L. S. (1987). *The collected works of L. S. Vygotsky, Vol. 1: Problems of general psychology.* Plenum Press.

Wald, P. J., & Castleberry, M. S. (2000). *Educators as learners: Creating a professional learning community in your school.* ASCD.

Waley, T. (2022). How can we tackle the teacher shortage?: Let's focus on retention. *Independence, 47*(2), 22–23. https://search.informit.org/doi/10.3316/informit.662023801240164

Ward, V. S. (1961). *Educating the gifted: An axiomatic approach.* C. E. Merrill Books.

Weldon, P. (2018). Early career teacher attrition in Australia: Evidence, definition, classification and measurement. *Australian Journal of Education, 62*(1), 61–78. https://doi.org/10.1177/0004944117752478

Westbroek, H. B., van Rens, L., van den Berg, E., & Janssen, F. (2020). A practical approach to assessment for learning and differentiated instruction. *International Journal of Science Education, 42*(6), 955–76. https://doi.org/10.1080/09500693.2020.1744044

Westwood, P. (2016). *What teachers need to know about differentiated instruction.* ACER Press.

Wiggins, G. P., & McTighe, J. (2005). *Understanding by design.* ASCD.

Wiggins, G. P., & McTighe, J. (2011). *The understanding by design guide to creating high-quality units.* ASCD.

Yoon, K. S., Duncan, T., Lee, S. W.-Y., Scarloss, B., & Shapley, K. (2007). Reviewing the evidence on how teacher professional development affects student achievement. Issues & answers. REL 2007-No. 033. *Regional Educational Laboratory Southwest.* https://eric.ed.gov/?id=ED498548

Milton Keynes UK
Ingram Content Group UK Ltd.
UKHW020638290424
441924UK00007B/560